The

COMPLETE BOOK OF

JERKY

© 2015 Quarto Publishing Group USA Inc.
Text © 2015 Philip Hasheider

First published in 2015 by Voyageur Press, an imprint of Quarto Publishing Group USA Inc., 400 First Avenue North, Suite 400, Minneapolis, MN 55401 USA. Telephone: (612) 344-8100 Fax: (612) 344-8692

quartoknows.com
Visit our blogs at quartoknows.com

Voyageur Press titles are also available at discounts in bulk quantity for industrial or sales-promotional use.
For details contact the Special Sales Manager at Quarto Publishing Group USA Inc., 400 First Avenue North, Suite 400, Minneapolis, MN 55401 USA.

10 9 8 7 6 5 4 3 2 1

ISBN: 978-0-7603-4914-4

Library of Congress Cataloging-in-Publication Data

Hasheider, Philip, 1951-
The complete book of jerky : how to process, prepare, and dry beef, venison, turkey, fish, and more / Philip Hasheider.
    pages cm
ISBN 978-0-7603-4914-4 (paperback)
1. Dried meat. I. Title.
TX749.H237 2015
664'.902--dc23
                        2015023657

Acquiring Editor: Thom O'Hearn
Project Manager: Caitlin Fultz
Art Director: James Kegley
Layout: Kim Winscher

Printed in China

Photo Credits
Shutterstock: Jiri Hera, 4, 58, 138; wavebreakmedia, 10; Tyler Olson, 30; JIANG HONGYAN, 116. *iStock*: 74, 98.

The COMPLETE BOOK OF JERKY

HOW TO PROCESS, PREPARE AND DRY BEEF, VENISON, TURKEY, FISH AND MORE

PHILIP HASHEIDER

CONTENTS

INTRODUCTION

When the first Europeans arrived in the New World, they discovered a food made of dried meat. It was developed by the indigenous peoples from any kind of meat they hunted that could not be immediately eaten. The Spanish explorers called it *charque* and it later became Anglicized for easier pronunciation as *jerky*.

Whether the meat came from buffalo, elk, fish, or other game, it was cut into strips and hung on racks to dry in the sun. Dehydrating these strips removed the water and made them lighter and easier for transport for their nomadic lifestyle while preserving them for emergency rations if fresh meat was not available.

Some Native American Indian tribes added animal fat, dried fruits, and berries, or all three to develop *pemmican*. Early European explorers quickly learned to make pemmican to supplement their diets in times of lean hunting success. The meat used by explorers and Native Americans contained no preservatives, was often low in fat and carbohydrates, and became one of the highest protein-concentrated foods available aside from fresh meat. For example, research has suggested that if a fur trade paddler required 7 to 10 pounds of meat consumed per day to sustain him, 1.5 to 2 pounds of pemmican would provide the equivalent nutrition. It yielded calories in an easily portable, compact form that made it suitable for long-term use.

When viewed from our nutritional context today, dried meat and berries supply not only protein but also the vitamins essential to fend off scurvy and fat as a ready source of energy. While the early explorers and travelers may not have considered it in those terms, they recognized it for their situation as an ideal food staple. They needed a high-energy food that could sustain them in lean hunting times and inclement weather conditions and keep them from starving.

Fast forward several hundred years, and jerky can be viewed today in a similar light. Although modern tastes have changed much from those explorer days, pemmican is still regarded as a survival food by those traveling in remote wilderness regions. Jerky itself is even more popular. There are many commercial varieties available, and it can be easily and safely processed at home from many kinds of meat. With our unprecedented access to spices and flavorings, we can produce a staggering variety of jerky flavors.

Beef jerky has become a popular snack. It is lightweight, portable, and provides protein and energy for active lifestyles.

Jerky is typically made of meat derived from beef.

One factor that makes jerky attractive to a wide variety of sportsmen, sportswomen, and even non-hunters is that almost any type of meat can be dried into jerky. Whether it derives from game animals such as deer, elk, or squirrel, or from domestic livestock such as cattle or poultry, their meat can be fashioned and dried into jerky. Wild game birds such as turkeys, pheasants, ducks, and geese are sources for jerky. It can be made from fresh or frozen fish. And it's possible to make jerky from soybean or plant-based products. The range is seemingly endless, and this provides a vast array of options to you.

Making jerky does not need to be the sole province of an outdoors or hunting lifestyle. The principles of jerky making are relatively simple and can be mastered by those willing to spend the time to study and adhere to proper food-handling techniques and the disciplines of safe food production. Its simplicity comes with a responsibility to follow processing recommendations that will create a safe and stable food product. With access to appropriate equipment you can make your own jerky.

The Complete Book of Jerky will guide you through the processing methods of making safe and satisfying jerky products for you and your family.

REASONS FOR MAKING JERKY

There are about as many different reasons for making jerky as there are people who make it. Like with other foods, a person's motivation for making jerky often depends on taste, variety, access to meat and equipment, and the amount of control they want over the manner their food is processed or preserved.

The food pyramid suggests a daily intake of carbohydrates, proteins, and fats to maintain a healthy body. These can be supplied by cereals, fruits and vegetables, milk, or meats. Many of these same foods can be used in jerky making to supply one or more of these requirements. Because jerky is often made from lean cuts of meat that are low in fat and cholesterol—a dense, concentrated source of nutrients—it can be a high protein and energy source.

Although some people have considered homemade jerky to be a less-expensive alternative to "store-bought" or "ready-made" products, for true cost comparisons you will need to factor in such things as equipment purchases, ingredient costs, and your time.

Jerky can also be easily made from wild game such as deer, moose, or elk. *Jim Ruen*

Jerky goes well with other foods, whether you are camping, hiking, or sitting in your backyard. *Jim Ruen*

But with some guidance, you can make jerky products that rival the expense and taste of those produced commercially, and you will have a homemade product.

HOW TO USE THIS BOOK

The purpose of this book is to help guide you through all aspects of making jerky, from sourcing the meat to processing it. Detailed discussion and step-by-step instructions will allow you to safely transform raw meat into a stable, edible snack or a meal side dish.

Different species and meat cuts from which jerky can be sourced are discussed in detail. You will learn about basic charcuterie or the cutting up of the meat into a manageable form before it is processed or dehydrated.

The numerous recipes included will help you make use of your jerky, but these represent only a fraction of what you can do with your jerky meats or how it can be processed into an attractive dish to serve at your family table. While recipes are located throughout the chapters by variety, they are meant to be used in tandem with the rest of the book—notably Chapters 1 through 3 and the four methods for making jerky that begin on page 60.

In short, this book can help you discover new food experiences. So, take a seat, turn the page, and we're off on a new adventure.

Chapter 1
GETTING STARTED

As with any new hobby, it may be tempting to jump right into making jerky, learning as you go and not fully understanding the basic steps. However, there's a reason jerky making is often not part of more general preservation books. There are additional considerations and very clear food safety recommendations that must be followed to ensure a safe food product.

I'm sure you agree, it is worth the time it takes to think about and learn the basic principles of food safety. After all, nothing is more important than you and your family's health. These basics include sanitation; factors affecting moisture, oxygen, temperature, and time; preventing and retarding bacterial growth; and muscle basics that can contribute to jerky's overall quality.

In addition to understanding good food-processing techniques, you should develop a plan for acquiring the tools and equipment needed to adequately process the meat into a safe, quality finished product. Your plan and equipment needs should be thought out long before you have the meat in hand, so that's where we're starting in this chapter.

JERKY AND FOOD SAFETY

The most important aspect of making jerky is to consider all the points where meat contamination may occur and to ensure contamination doesn't happen. Preventing food-borne illnesses should always be your top priority.

Unless you're making vegan jerky, you will start with raw meat or fish either harvested in the wild or purchased at a local meat counter. There are basic steps you can take to ensure safe handling of raw meat cuts that will minimize the risks involved with processing it. You may already be familiar with the three standard "Cs": keeping meat **C**lean, **C**old, and **C**overed. There's one additional "C" I like to include as well: keeping meat separate to prevent **C**ross-contamination.

Note: One other significant consideration to be made once the meat is ready to be processed is to cook it or heat it to the appropriate temperature, but that comes into play later in its own section (see page 16).

Keep It Clean

Let's start with keeping things clean. Strict sanitation is required before and after cutting any meat—whether in the wild or in your home—and processing it into jerky to prevent bacterial contamination and food-borne illnesses. It is especially important to handle raw meat in a sanitary environment to reduce the risk of bacterial growth while it is at room temperature. No meat is completely sterile, but using proper procedures will minimize your risks.

The greatest challenge for maintaining sanitation occurs when harvesting and field dressing game animals in the wild. Domestic animals are raised under controlled environments that have protocols to guide producers in raising healthy animals for the market. Their meat is processed under strict

Cleanliness is very important when handling raw meat, regardless of if it is sourced from a store or the wild. Safe food processing begins with washing your hands thoroughly with soap and water prior to handling any meat.

Use rubber or latex gloves when handling or field dressing wild game. Gloves act as a barrier between your skin and an animal's body fluids in case of any unseen infections.

Remove all rings and watches from your hands and wrists before working with raw meats to avoid the introduction of bacteria.

Field Dressing as Cleanly as Possible

For many years, it was thought that the muscle of an animal was sterile if it had not been injured, cut into, or bruised. However, recent research has found viable bacteria within muscle tissue. This means that when you harvest an animal, especially in the wild, extreme care must be taken to prevent the introduction of foreign bodies into the carcass through your actions. This care begins with the knives and equipment you use during the meat processing and continues until the meat has been dried for use.

Successful hunting typically results in wounds made from bullets, arrows, or hooks. These create openings in muscles and body cavities, which can become contaminated. Portions of the carcass may have materials embedded such as hair, dirt, metal shards, and any mixture of blood, bone chips, and fecal matter. All damaged tissue needs to be cut out and removed. Your knife should be sterilized before and after excising the wound area or digging out a bullet or arrow tip. Be aware that bullet or arrow fragments may splinter and be embedded in areas not readily observed and may pass deep into muscles without leaving a noticeable path. These pieces may be too small to be seen and may be dispersed away from the wound channel. Any wound area should be excised as soon as possible to prevent bacterial growth from spreading into the muscles.

Still, the most exposure a wild game carcass has to its environmental conditions occurs during field dressing. Whether it is a deer, squirrel, elk, moose, or rabbit that has been killed, its surroundings typically include dirt, dust, plants, insects, and depending on the time of year, atmospheric temperature concerns. It is vitally important to minimize carcass contamination from the elements present by using as many precautions as possible. This could include using plastic sheeting on which to lay a carcass while making any initial cuts. Try to refrain from using water from creeks or streams to flush out any body cavity. Water in the field may contain bacteria or soil particles that can contaminate the meat and lead to an excellent environment for bacterial growth.

If you decide to or need to field dress your game animal, you should always wear protective gloves, either rubber or latex, especially when dressing and skinning some game such as wild rabbits or hares. This will protect you from possible contact with a communicable disease known as tularemia, or rabbit fever. This is a very infectious disease that can be transmitted from one rabbit to another by lice or ticks, or to humans by handling the flesh of an infected animal, inhaling the bacteria during the skinning process, or through a tick bite. Since its entry is through cuts, abrasions, or inhalation, you need to take precautions. You may not recognize an infected animal prior to skinning it, so strict sanitation is essential.

sanitary conditions before it is sold to another market or grocery store. Wild game does not have such guidelines and health regulations.

Cleanliness and sanitation also play a significant role when indoors. This includes using and maintaining clean knives and work counters or cutting surfaces; ensuring proper insect, fly, and rodent control; and frequent hand washing.

Cleaning is the first step before sanitizing. Cleaning involves removing any organic matter by using detergents, solvent cleaners, acid, and/or abrasive cleaners as necessary. Sanitizing follows and is the application of heat or chemicals, typically a chlorine-based solution, to surfaces that will come in contact with food.

Whatever you use for a cutting surface must be cleaned thoroughly and then sanitized before placing any meat on it to prevent contamination. Vigorous scrubbing may be necessary and cleaning products should remove any grease or unwanted contaminants from the preparation area before sanitation. If they don't, you should repeat the cleaning process. All the utensils that you will use should be cleaned before they're sanitized as well.

For a sanitizer, mix a solution of 1 part chlorine bleach to 10 parts water and use it to wash the surface of your table, cutting board, or counter. You can use this solution to briefly soak any tools, knives, or other equipment that will contact meat and then rinse these with clear, clean water before use.

Another option is to use an acid-based, no-rinse sanitizer such as Star San. This is a commercially available cleaner that is odorless and flavorless and will eliminate any concerns about tainting your meat. Although chlorine reacts quickly and becomes inactive quickly, you should always follow the mixing directions exactly. Spray the surface of your table, cutting board, or counter with this solution and use a small bucket or bowl to soak any tools.

Keep your work area clean and free of any items not involved with your food processing. A simple cleaning solution can be used.

Clean all work surfaces thoroughly and wipe dry before placing raw meat on them.

Wash all knives that you will use with hot, soapy water or other cleaning solution and then rinse with clean, clear water. Be sure to thoroughly clean the joint where the blade attaches to the handle.

Note: **It's always a good idea to remove any materials or equipment that will not be used in the meat preparation from your work area. If they are not being used, they may become a hindrance in your work space and should be treated as contaminated if you have to move them while you are cutting the meat.**

Any knife being considered for use in cutting meat should be thoroughly washed before and after each use. Use mild soapy water and clean by hand. When cleaning knives that are more than one solid piece, you should pay close attention to the area where the blade attaches to the handle. This is an area where meat or blood residue will remain after cutting and is an ideal habitat for microorganisms to grow later as knives are generally stored at room temperature. Remember, if it's not clean, it can't be sanitized.

Other equipment that may be used, including slicers, meat grinders, extruders, rolling pins, presses, scales, or other utensils, should also be thoroughly washed prior to each use. They can also be sanitized in a chlorine bleach solution as an added precaution, but be sure to thoroughly rinse each piece separately in clear, clean water before using to remove any possible chlorine tainting of the meat.

The type of material you use to clean counter or cutting board surfaces can be a concern. Sponges and wet cloths are typically used for cleaning and when used properly can do an excellent job. However, bacteria live and grow in damp conditions, and wet sponges and cloths make ideal harbors for foodborne pathogens. Sponges and cloths that give off unpleasant odors are a sure sign that unsafe bacteria are present.

Sponges can be used successfully if properly cleaned. You can't eliminate all of the bacteria that may reside in sponges, but you can reduce the risk of cross-contamination and the spread of harmful bacteria by following a few easy steps.

- First, clean your sponges daily. It will lower the risk of bacterial growth. The USDA has found that by microwave-heating damp sponges for 1 minute or dishwashing with a drying cycle will kill over 99 percent of the bacteria, yeasts, and molds present. You can also disinfect sponges with a solution of ¼ to ½ teaspoon of concentrated bleach per quart of warm water and a soak of a minimum of 1 minute.

- Second, replace sponges frequently. This will reduce bacterial growth. Frequent use of any sponge can develop pockets that harbor bacteria even when routinely cleaned. Don't wait until the sponge falls apart before tossing it away. A clean sponge is a safe sponge.

- Third, store your cleaning sponges in a dry place. Wring them out completely after each use and wash off any loose food or debris. Don't allow them to remain wet on a countertop because this will mean they will dry more slowly, which will allow bacteria to multiply quickly. Don't store damp sponges under a sink or in a bucket where they won't be exposed to circulating air.

Dishtowels and cloths should be handled in the same way as sponges. Keeping them disinfected and dry, while periodically replacing them, will help keep bacterial growth to a minimum. You should also use separate towels or cloths: one for drying hands and one for wiping counters. Remember to wash them in hot water and dry them on high heat in your dryer.

Whenever possible, you should clean up spills with disposable paper towels rather than using sponges or cloths for such small tasks to avoid cross-contamination.

Once everything is ready, it's a good idea to thoroughly wash your hands with soap and water before touching any meat or clean work surfaces. Remove any rings, jewelry, or other metal objects from your hands, ears, or other exposed body parts before cutting meat. Always rewash your hands between tasks, as well as if you come into contact with anything unsanitary: if you sneeze, use the bathroom, or handle materials not part of meat processing, you should rewash your hands.

Keep It Cold (and/or Hot)

Mismanagement of temperature is one of the most common reasons for outbreaks of food-borne diseases. Bacteria grow best at temperatures between 40 degrees and 140 degrees Fahrenheit, so it is important that your meat product passes through this range quickly. Meat can be kept safe when it is hot or when it is cold, but not in between. It is best if the meat passes through this temperature range, whether being cooked or cooled, within four hours, but preferably less. This includes both domestic and wild game animal meats. Cooling a wild game carcass quickly is essential to a good meat product.

Store your raw meat in a refrigerator until you begin processing it. During the processing of most meat products, it will be essential to reach an internal temperature of 160 degrees Fahrenheit, as this effectively kills pathogenic bacteria. (Most, but not all, microorganisms are killed at 140 degrees Fahrenheit.) The interior of the meat can be considered sterile, or nearly so, unless it has been cut into.

Prior to processing or dehydrating your jerky, it is likely you will be working with a raw meat product for a period of time. The less time you subject the meat to room or ambient temperatures, the less risk there will be in it harboring harmful microorganisms that cause spoilage. This is especially true if the meat in question has been harvested in the wild where temperature and time will affect its quality more than if purchased in a store.

If meat is stored below 40 degrees Fahrenheit, most of it can be kept safe from harmful bacteria for a short time. When frozen, most microorganisms that are present are merely dormant and can revive when thawed. If you have thawed the meat you plan to use for jerky, it all should be processed as soon as possible and not refrozen to use for jerky later.

Temperature remains the critical factor once you proceed to jerky production. In decades past, the standard was for the meat to be heated between 130 to 140 degrees Fahrenheit, which many dehydrators could achieve. However, the current United States Department of Agriculture (USDA) recommendation for safe jerky making is to heat meat to 160 degrees Fahrenheit (and poultry to 165 degrees Fahrenheit) before the dehydrating process begins. Reaching these temperatures will assure that the wet heat will destroy any bacteria present. Research has shown that without reaching these temperatures before dehydrating, any bacteria present after drying become more heat resistant and may survive in sufficient quantities to create health problems later. We'll learn more about this on page 19.

Keep It Covered

All foods have a diminishing shelf life after they are opened or made, even if properly stored. However, the manner in which you cover, contain, or wrap foods prior to use or storage determines how well it keeps in a refrigerator, cupboard, or freezer.

Temperature has the greatest effect on meat, especially as it increases. As previously mentioned, raw or cooked meat should be kept chilled until used. Even your refrigerator will not have consistent temperatures throughout. Interior drawers tend to have slightly higher temperatures than shelves. The door shelves are also generally warmer because of their exposure to room temperatures once they are opened. So it's best not to store highly perishable foods such as meat in the drawers or doors of your refrigerator.

Wrapping or enclosing foods in containers will help keep them fresher than if left uncovered in the refrigerator. Uncovered meat has more exposure to oxygen, which can cause bacteria to multiply faster. Oxygen also tends to dry out the meat surface much quicker.

Wrapping or containing meat serves several purposes. It forms a barrier between the meat and oxygen, it prevents refrigerator odors from transferring from one food to another, and it helps prevent cross-contamination between foods that may occur through drips or touch. Outside the refrigerator, wrapped or covered meats are less exposed to flies, insects, or pets.

There are a number of products you can use to wrap, cover, and store your foods, and each has its advantages.

- Aluminum foil is good for keeping moisture out of food, and it protects food from light and oxygen. It has reactive properties, however, and shouldn't be used with acidic foods such as berries or tomatoes. A layer of plastic wrap followed by a layer of aluminum foil will provide a double protective layer for any food. It is also very good for use in freezing foods.

- Plastic wrap provides close to an airtight seal on bowls and containers without lids. It has a unique ability to adhere to a variety of surfaces, whether plastic or glass. Because it is transparent, you can see what's inside without having to open the package. Don't use or leave plastic wrap on any container or food being heated or cooked.

- Resealable plastic bags come in a variety of sizes and weights (thicknesses). The heavier-weight bags are good for freezing foods. They provide the best protection when the air is pressed out of the bag prior to sealing it.

- Airtight glass or plastic containers with lids can be cooled or frozen. Some, such as Pyrex containers or other shatterproof types, can be used in either cold or boiling water.

- Freezer paper is a plastic-coated paper designed for wrapping foods destined for the freezer. It is much heavier material than aluminum foil or plastic wrap and provides good protection for storing foods. You can also write on it so that you know what is inside.

- Waxed paper is a moisture-proof material that is made by applying wax to the paper surface. It has a slightly higher heat tolerance than plastic wrap but should not be used in cooking or baking. Its nonstick surface properties make it a good barrier between frozen food cuts wrapped in the same package.

- Parchment paper is often used in heating or baking because of its ability to withstand oven heat without combusting (except if it comes into contact with the burner coils). It can be used to act as a barrier between foods you are working with on your table or cutting board, or between cuts of meats you want to freeze in the same package so they will separate with little trouble. Parchment paper can be used to line pans or trays for quick clean up.

- Vacuum sealers are appliances that remove all the air from any package being sealed, which will extend the shelf life of the food inside (not indefinitely) and decrease the chance of freezer burn. Vacuum-sealed packages can be stored in your refrigerator, freezer, or cupboard, depending on the type of food sealed.

Preventing Cross-Contamination

Cross-contamination occurs when one food comes in contact with another, creating the potential of spreading bacteria from one source to another. One or both foods might be raw, or one can be raw and one cooked. Cross-contamination can occur when foods touch, or it can occur when surfaces have had mutual contact with several foods, such as when one food is placed on a plate, counter, or cutting board, then removed, and then another food is placed on the same now-contaminated surface. It can also occur between knives that have not been cleaned between uses, and even in your grocery cart if juices happen to leak from one package to another.

There are several steps you can take to avoid cross-contamination of any foods.

- Always wash your hands thoroughly with warm, soapy water prior to, during, and after handling raw meats and other foods. Make sure all counters, cutting boards, plates, knives, and other utensils are thoroughly washed and dried with clean towels.

- Separate different foods into different dishes, plates, or bowls prior to use.

- Keep raw meat, poultry, seafood, or eggs on the bottom shelf of your refrigerator and in sealed containers or bags so they cannot leak or drip onto another food.

- Use a clean cutting board for each of the different foods you are working with. Use separate boards for raw meats, vegetables, and other foods. If you are using the same knives or equipment for all your cutting and processing,

Prevent cross-contamination by keeping different foods, such as meat and fish, separate from each other. Always clean the surface worked on prior to placing a different food on it.

Preventing and Retarding Bacterial Growth

Although sanitation and the three (or four) "C" dynamics have become routine components of jerky processing, misuse or incomplete application of any one of them can be detrimental. Preventing and retarding the development of harmful organisms should be your primary objective while handling raw meat and turning it into jerky. Consuming microorganisms that have grown and propagated in meat can cause serious illness or even death. This concern should not be taken lightly. When health problems surface relating to eating meat products, even if it's jerky that has been dehydrated, they are generally a result of intoxication or infection.

Intoxication occurs when heating or processing fails to kill the microbes in food. Those that are able to survive can produce a toxin that, when eaten by humans, can produce illness. In undercooked meat, for example, infection occurs when an organism such as salmonella or listeria is consumed.

There are several types of toxins, including exotoxins and endotoxins.

- Exotoxins are located outside of the bacterial cell and are composed of proteins that can be destroyed by heat through cooking. Exotoxins are among the most poisonous substances known to humans. These include *Clostridium botulinum*, which causes tetanus and botulism poisoning.

- Endotoxins attach to the outer membranes of cells but are not released unless the cell is disrupted. These are complex fat and carbohydrate molecules, such as *Staphylococcus aureus*, which are not destroyed by heat.

Not all bacteria are bad, however. According to one New York University study, the human body may carry as many as 180 different kinds of bacteria on its surface. Although molds and yeasts can affect meat quality and cause spoilage, their effect is far less significant or life-threatening

If using a wood cutting board, make certain that it is free from cracks or crevices that may harbor bacteria. Thoroughly clean your cutting board before and after each use.

wash them thoroughly each time you move from one food to another or from one cutting surface to another. Replace any cutting boards that have cracks, holes, or grooves, as these are good places for bacteria to hide and grow.

- Avoid using leftover marinade for any other meats. If you need the same marinade for another dish, set aside a small amount before placing raw meat in it. This will leave you with a fresh marinade for later use.

- Clean your refrigerator shelves on a regular basis, particularly if juices from raw meat, vegetables, or seafood have leaked, dripped, or spilled.

- Try to avoid mixing raw meat, vegetables, seafood, and eggs in the same bags when you check out at the grocery store. Try to separate frozen and fresh food into separate bags.

- Never place cooked food on a plate that was used for raw meat, poultry, seafood, or eggs.

than toxins or bacteria. Molds typically cause spoilage in grains, cereals, flour, and nuts that have low moisture content or in fruits that have a low pH. Yeasts will not have a significant effect on meat because of the low sugar or carbohydrate content of muscle. They need high sugar and carbohydrate levels to affect a change.

Several parasites may cause problems if the meat being used for jerky is undercooked or improperly processed. A parasite infection occurs first in the live animal and then, after butchering, may be transferred to humans while still in an active state. There are three parasites that you should be aware of, depending on which meat you decide to use for jerky. These include *Trichinella spiralis*, *Toxoplasma gondii,* and *Anisakis marina.*

- *Trichinella* is a parasite that can live in swine muscle and may be transferred to humans through raw or undercooked pork.

- *Toxoplasma* is a small protozoan that occurs throughout the world and has been observed in a wide range of birds and mammals.

- *Anisakis* is a roundworm parasite found only in fish. Using and maintaining recommended cooking temperatures and time will destroy these parasites.

One disease that may be a concern is chronic wasting disease (CWD). It is a progressive, fatal illness in deer, elk, and moose. It has attracted attention because it has been identified in animals in fifteen United States and two Canadian provinces. CWD is believed to be caused by a prion protein that damages portions of the brain in affected animals. It causes progressive loss of body condition, behavioral changes, excessive salivation, and finally, death. The mode of transmission is not fully understood, but it is thought that the disease is spread through direct contact between animals or exposure to contaminated water and food supplies.

As of this writing, no strong evidence of CWD transmission to humans has been reported. Still, hunters harvesting animals originating in known CWD-positive areas should have them tested before consuming any of the meat, regardless of whether it will be made into jerky. You can take precautions prior to harvesting an animal by not shooting, handling, or eating any deer, elk, or moose that appears sick or decimated or tests positive for CWD. Also, if you field dress one of these cervids, it is a good precaution to wear gloves, bone-out the meat from the carcass, and minimize handling of the brain and spinal cord tissues (for more on this, see page 87).

Moisture and Oxygen

Moisture in meat is essential for palatability but is also a medium for microbial growth. The level of moisture in fresh meat is high enough to provide spoilage organisms with an ideal environment for growth. Researchers have found that moisture levels of at least 18 percent will allow molds to grow in meat. Drying meats through a smoking process or by making it into jerky will typically eliminate any concerns with moisture.

Oxygen is an unwelcome agent when processing meats. Yeasts and molds are aerobic microbes that need oxygen to grow. Anaerobic microbes grow when oxygen is not present, and this group can be deadly because they include clostridium, which produces a toxin, and a group called *putrifiers*, which degrades proteins and produces foul-smelling gases.

Drying is the safest procedure to follow when making homemade jerky because it acts as an inhibitor of enzyme action by removing moisture. When moisture is removed, enzymes cannot efficiently contact or react with the meat fibers or particles. Without this interaction, bacteria, fungal spores, or naturally occurring enzymes from the raw meat cannot grow to proportions that can cause severe illness. Minute traces may still be present, but with no growth, they lie dormant.

However, lying dormant does not mean they can't resume growth if favorable moisture or temperature conditions are introduced. This may occur if jerky is left out in moist conditions and is one important reason to keep any homemade jerky in cool, dry conditions until eaten.

Eating jerky that has been made with sanitary practices carries minimum risks, for several reasons. First, the high internal temperature that is created (to be discussed in detail later) significantly reduces the survival of salmonella, *E. coli*, trichinosis, and other bacteria. Additionally, processing jerky typically involves using more salt than you would use with many other uncooked foods for your table. Salt acts as an inhibitor of bacterial growth but also adds flavor after the meat is dried. Third, drying can eliminate more than 90 percent of the meat's water content, a medium needed for bacterial growth.

Muscles and Molecular Transformation

Muscles are meat. The position of the muscles on the skeleton has a significant impact on the texture of meat. For example, muscles that create movement—such as the front and hind quarters in herbivores such as cattle, pigs, and sheep, or the wings and thighs of wild turkeys—receive more exercise than the loin or breast areas of these animals and fowl. The more exercise or movement a muscle uses, the more blood flow is needed. This, in turn, creates a darker color of meat because of the flow of hemoglobin needed to deliver oxygen to the muscle. The more hemoglobin (sometimes referred to as myoglobin) a muscle contains,

the darker color the muscle will be. In fish, the large muscles of the body and tail comprise the majority of the body mass and because they provide the most movement, they will contain the most blood. The muscles that receive the most use for movement typically also contain the least amount of fat because the fat is synthesized by the muscle for energy. Muscles with little fat also tend to be less tender in texture and, ultimately, in taste. Although any meat cut can be used, jerky is often made from the less desirable cuts as a way of using rather than discarding them.

The muscles of a harvested animal or bird, whether field dressed or butchered in a confined indoor area, go through a molecular transformation once the heart stops. This can influence the muscle texture. With the cessation of blood and oxygen flow, the muscle pH begins to gradually drop. This occurs because the glycogen reserves within the animal's muscles are depleted and are converted to lactic acid. Lactic acid levels rise, the pH begins to drop, and the reserves of creatine phosphates diminish. Creatine phosphates aid in muscle movement; when they are no longer available, the muscle filaments can no longer slide over one another and the muscle becomes still and rigid, resulting in a condition known as *rigor mortis*.

Soon after an animal is harvested, the muscle's normal pH declines from 7.0 to 5.5 as a result of the loss of glycogen held in the muscle and its conversion to lactic acid. The degree of acidity or alkalinity (pH) will have an effect on the growth of microorganisms. Most of these will thrive at a pH that is nearly neutral (7.0), better than at any other level above or below it. Meat pH can range from 4.8 to 6.8, but microorganisms generally grow slower at a pH of 5.0 or below. This acidity level can act as a preservative in some instances and is generally not a concern unless there is a long delay in processing the carcass at room temperatures.

The amount of time it takes an animal's muscles to reach their final pH levels is influenced by several factors. These include the species, cooling rate of the carcass, and the extent of the animal's struggle at the time of death. Deer muscles take longer to reach their final pH level than many other wild animals. Cooling affects the time because metabolism is slowed when the carcass is subjected to lower temperatures. Finally, the animal's activity level immediately prior to the killing will affect the pH, with less activity prolonging the period of pH decline.

TOOLS AND PREPARATION

You have learned to keep your raw meat safe from harvest to processing. You have learned to avoid contamination, spoilage, and bacterial growth that affects quality and health, and why meat decreases in quality as time goes by. What else do you need to know? Understanding your work and storage space needs and the equipment you will use will get you ready for the chapters that follow.

The good news is that elaborate working areas are not required to make jerky. A solid table with sturdy legs or a stable counter space can be made into suitable areas to cut meat. Whatever surface area you use, make sure it can be easily cleaned and that it's made of nonporous material that will not harbor food residue. Using a hard, even surface will make cutting meat easy and safe.

Home-use cutting boards are typically made of nonmetallic materials such as solid plastic, marble, glass, or rubber, and are generally corrosion-resistant. Their nonporous surfaces are easier to clean than wood, but if kept in good condition, wood boards can work as well.

The USDA Food Safety and Inspection Service recommends that all cutting boards used in your home first be cleaned with hot, soapy water before and after each use and then rinsed with clear water and either air dried or patted dry with clean paper towels. It also recommends that separate cutting boards be used for meats and vegetables.

Your preparation should also include gathering cleaning and sanitizing supplies. There is a wide variety of products available and there is no single detergent that is capable of removing all types of soils or complex films that may be a combination of food components, surface oils, or dust. Common cleaning agents include detergents such as dishwashing liquids that alter the physical and chemical characteristics of the substances being cleaned to neutralize and degrade them; solvent cleaners such as ammonia that contain grease-dissolving agents; acid cleaners such as hydrochloric acid that can remove mineral deposits that alkaline detergents cannot; and abrasive cleaners such as fine steel wool, copper, or nylon. Sanitizing compounds include antiseptics that are used against toxic agents or bacteria that may cause infections or have a putrefaction effect; disinfectants or germicides that are applied to stationary objects such as floors and countertops and will kill vegetative cells but not spores; and bactericides that can be used to kill certain groups of microorganisms but, depending on the type or strain, may only prevent their growth.

Sanitizers that include chlorine bleach, hydrogen peroxide, or white distilled vinegar, either in diluted or undiluted concentrations, are effective on food preparation surfaces. However, don't use baking soda because it is not an effective sanitizer at any temperature, time, or concentration. Using a combination of heat and chemicals is the best way to make food preparation surfaces and equipment safe and to help avoid food contamination.

Nonmetallic containers, glass bowls, measuring cups and spoons, and paper towels are some items that will be useful while making jerky.

For making jerky, there are a few essential tools you need to buy if you don't already have them in your kitchen. We'll cover the key items in detail on the pages that follow. You'll also want to make sure your kitchen has the following basics: measuring cups and spoons, glass bowls or other non-metallic containers for marinades, containers or other packaging materials for finished jerky, plastic bags or plastic wrap, and kitchen towels and paper towels. Also, if you're planning to use your oven in the jerky-making process, you'll need to make sure you have clean and sturdy oven racks as well as cookie sheets and foil.

Of course, you'll also need to decide whether you'll be using your oven, a dehydrator, and/

or a smoker. The tools you use for drying are tightly integrated with drying techniques. We will discuss them all in their own chapter starting on page 58. No matter which method you use, though, you will need the tools and equipment on the following pages.

Cold Storage Space

As already discussed, temperature is a primary factor you should control during meat processing and preservation. You should make sure the meat you use, whether harvested or purchased, is kept below 40 degrees Fahrenheit until your processing begins. For small batches of jerky, you should have no problems using your fridge. However, should you scale up or bring home a large amount of meat from a hunting trip, you need to make sure you have the dedicated fridge space ready.

Although properly processed jerky needs little refrigeration, it is advisable to keep your finished product in a cool, dry place. Keeping jerky in a refrigerated or frozen state will lengthen the time it will be available to you. To keep it for an extended period in a freezer, it will be best to have it vacuum packed to reduce the formation of ice crystals, which can reduce the meat quality. A vacuum packer removes the air from the package prior to sealing, which prevents the invasion of moisture, so it can be a good way to extend the life of jerky even if you don't plan to freeze it. Remember that even if you freeze jerky, improper jerky processing may not have removed all bacteria from the meat. The harmful bacteria may be reactivated once the jerky is thawed out. It is essential that only properly processed jerky meats be frozen for consumption later.

Knives

You will need knives to cut your meat into strips prior to drying for jerky. Even if you plan to use a meat slicer, chances are you will need a good, sharp knife to trim your cut of meat before slicing it.

Your knife collection can range from simple, folding combination knives to a larger, sturdy straight knife. Use knives that fit your purpose, are sharp and sturdy, and are easily cleaned.

If you need to purchase a knife, there are several things to consider. First, one knife may be able to perform multiple tasks such as slicing large or small pieces of meat, but you may find a couple of different, more specialized knives make the task easier. For example, a wide-bladed knife works well for slicing meat into thin strips for jerky making or into chunks for grinding into ground jerky. But thin-bladed, flexible knives are easier to use in deboning meat in preparation for jerky slices.

Knives can come with wooden or plastic handles, have flexible or stiff blades, and come in many sizes and shapes. Wood-handled knives should not be cleaned in a dishwasher while plastic knives might be. The high water temperature may affect the temper of metal-bladed knives so that they will not hold their edge later when sharpened.

Try to buy knives that are sharp, easy to maintain, and keep a sharp edge.

Always keep your knives clean, whether in use or not. Unsanitary knives may harbor harmful organisms that can ultimately affect your health. Clean your knives before and after each use. You can use a mild soapy water solution and clean them by hand.

Shelf-Stable Jerky

The USDA defines "shelf stable" as food that can be safely stored at room temperature or "on the shelf." These are non-perishable products that can include jerky, rice, pasta, flour, and sugar. Foods that can't be kept safe at room temperature, such as seafood, milk, and raw meats, are labeled "keep refrigerated."

A requirement to be shelf stable is that the perishable food must be treated by heat and/or dried to destroy food-borne microorganisms that can cause illness or spoil food. Foods with this designation can be packaged in sterile, airtight containers. It is a standard rule that if not preserved in some manner, all foods will eventually spoil.

Many different types of knives can be used for cutting meat. Regardless of the ones you select, make sure they are sturdy, easy to clean, and sharp.

If your meat knife is to be stored for a long period between uses, you should check it periodically for any reddish spots that may show early signs of tarnish or oxidation. These early rust signs can harbor microorganisms and bacteria that may affect the meat the next time you use it. You should clean the blade before further use. Stainless-steel blades are not rustproof, although most are rust and stain resistant.

Knife Blades and Sharpening
In what at first appears a contradiction in terms, a sharp knife is the safest knife to use. This is because sharp knives cut more easily than dull knives, making the cut easier and safer. Less effort and pressure is required to cut through the meat with a sharp knife than a dull one, thereby reducing the risk of the blade

Simple Knife Rules

- Always use a sharp knife when cutting meat.
- Never hold a knife under your arm or leave it under a piece of meat.
- Keep knives visible.
- Always keep the knife point down.
- Always cut down toward the cutting surface and away from your body.
- Never leave children unattended around knives.
- Clean knives thoroughly before storing them safely.
- Always wash knives when switching between food items.

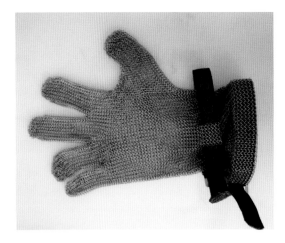

A mesh glove is interlaced with metal strips to prevent the blade from passing through the cloth. It provides protection in case the knife slips while cutting meat and is typically used on the hand not holding the knife. Be sure to thoroughly clean a mesh glove before and after each use with hot, soapy water.

slipping off what you're cutting unexpectedly and causing injury.

A knife with a high-carbon steel blade is best. This is a blade with about 0.5 percent carbon. If the blade is made with too little carbon, it will be soft and the edge of the knife may bend. If the carbon content is too high, it will be too hard and more difficult to sharpen. Try to find one that is hard enough to hold an edge but soft enough for easy resharpening at home when it becomes dull. This puts the blade with a Rockwell hardness rating of between 57 and 60. Many knives sold through commercial outlets are made to hold their edge. Older knives may not have those characteristics but may be useable if correctly sharpened. If you have the expertise, you can sharpen the knives yourself or they can be sharpened by someone who specializes in blades.

If you want to sharpen knives yourself, there are three basic steps: grinding, honing, and steeling. Each uses a different technique depending on the condition of the blade.

- Grinding gives the blade its thinness and will remove a small portion of the blade. Grinding produces a beveled or angled edge on the blade. The proper angle then can be honed. The basic purpose of grinding is to make one side of the blade meet the other side.

- Honing sharpens the beveled edge and requires a stone with a finer surface than a grinding stone.

- Steeling is the process that makes the edge perfectly straight by removing any burrs on the blade edge made in the grinding process or missed during honing. Burrs that remain on the blade will cause the meat to tear rather than be sliced. Steeling will realign the edge of the knife.

Keep your knives sharp, clean, and dry, and avoid storing them in places where they can get nicked or damaged by other objects. Always remember that there is an inherent danger in handling, using, and sharpening knives. Knife safety, particularly during sharpening, is a matter of common sense. If you go slowly, pay attention to detail, and stay focused, you should have little trouble.

Electric knives can be used in place of standard knives, but be sure your knife has an appropriate blade for the task. Any electric knife will need care and maintenance like other electric equipment and should be kept away from any water source while in use.

Gloves

Gloves are one of the best protections to use when cutting meat. Several different types of gloves will be useful and serve different purposes.

Rubber or latex gloves are essential when cutting up carcasses in the field because they will act as a barrier between you and the body fluids of wild game. However, they must be thoroughly washed and disinfected if not disposed of after each use.

Use a butchering glove when slicing meat in your home if you are unsure of your cutting technique or just prefer the extra safety measure. These gloves come in several sizes and are easy to wash. They are designed to be worn on the hand holding the meat, opposite of the hand holding a knife. Some gloves have braided stainless-steel threads woven into them. These prevent cuts and most punctures. Other types include a mesh glove that is made of solid stainless-steel rings that protect hands and fingers against cuts, slashes, and lacerations, but may not entirely stop punctures.

A mesh or butchering glove can be used in field dressing but, if used, you should still wear a rubber or latex glove underneath. A mesh glove is porous and fluids can seep through to your hand. Without a second barrier glove underneath, such as a rubber glove, the effect would be no different than working with your bare hands.

Kitchen Scale

An accurate kitchen scale is necessary for weighing and measuring the correct quantities

A digital scale accurately measures spices and meat quantities in jerky recipes.

of spices, flavorings, additives, cure, or anything else that will be mixed into or onto the meat. Of course, you'll also want to weigh your meat to make sure you're following the recipe. Spices and flavorings do not weigh very much, so you may want to consider obtaining a digital scale that accurately measures minute amounts. Typically, with the amounts and weights listed in the recipes contained in this book, a scale that can measure from ounces to a few pounds will cover most of your needs. These types of scales can range in price, but you should be able to find one that is affordable and accurate. Most standard scale models are easy to clean and should be readily available.

Thermometers

Eating undercooked meat always carries health risks. The best way to monitor the correct cooking temperatures is to use a thermometer that is accurate, durable, and easy to use. There are a variety of meat thermometers available with digital models becoming more popular.

Instant-read digital meat thermometers are simple to use, provide a fast response time when checking meat, work well for thin slices of meat, and can be used to check temperatures at several spots. While they are good for checking temperatures at different points of the cooking or drying cycle, most are not designed to remain in the meat during the cooking process.

A digital thermometer model that has a probe that can remain in the meat while it cooks is also something I recommend. Most feature a probe at the end of a long cord that connects to a base unit with a digital screen that is placed on a counter or can be attached to the outside of the oven door. Because the jerky strips are about ⅛ to ¼ inch in thickness, selecting a small, thin probe would work best, regardless of model.

Dial-stem thermometers can withstand high internal temperatures of dehydrators and ovens.

They are more difficult to use for determining the internal meat temperature of jerky because the stem is often too thick to insert into a meat strip. However, they are useful for measuring the internal oven and dehydrator temperatures to make sure they are high enough to cook the meat completely through.

Optional: Slicers

Jerky making can be aided with slicers and grinders, depending on your desire for speed and precision. Electric slicers can cut meat to an exact thickness and more evenly than you can likely do by hand and knife. There are many commercial models available with working parts that are easy to disassemble, clean, and put back together. They are relatively safe to use, and their variable thickness settings allow you to alter the jerky you wish to make. Like other cutting edges, the blades must be respected. The use of a mesh glove for the hand that passes the meat along the rotating blade will help protect you from inadvertent injury.

Optional: Grinders and Extruders

Ground meat can be made into jerky, but you will need a meat grinder (see pages 38–40 for more on this topic). Meat grinders come in a variety of models, from hand-cranked to electric. It is sometimes preferable to use a grinder that takes trimmings and odd-shaped pieces as they may be difficult to slice with a knife or meat slicer. Whether you use a hand-powered or electric grinder will likely depend on the amount of ground meat jerky you want to make. A grinder operated by hand is useful for small amounts while an electric grinder will save time for large quantities.

A meat extruder can be used in making jerky by forming the meat into round sticks or flat strips. It is a metal or plastic hand-held tube into which mixed ingredients of meat and additives are packed and then forced through an opening by a pressure plunger. The meat to be used is first ground to a desired consistency before flavorings and spices are mixed in. This mixture is then stuffed into the tube for dispensing. It is forced out the opposite end by the plunger and, through a special attachment or tip, can be formed into a flat strip or round stick shape to be dried. There are numerous commercial models available, ranging from hand pumps to electric varieties that can handle large batches of jerky meat.

A hand-powered slicer can be taken apart for easy cleaning. Wash all parts thoroughly with hot, soapy water before and after each use.

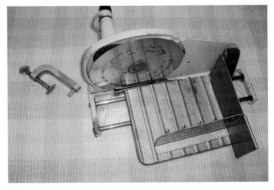

The reassembled meat slicer can be used instead of knives to create even slices.

Top left: A hand-cranked meat grinder is one type of grinder that can be used to break down small or odd pieces that can't be cut into strips.

Top right: A hand- or electric-powered meat grinder should be taken apart and all pieces should be thoroughly cleaned before and after each use.

Above: A variety of containers can be used to store meat prior to use. Keep all meats covered while in a refrigerator to prevent any cross-contamination from other foods or liquids.

Chapter 2
CUTTING AND PREPARING MEAT FOR JERKY

The range of meats you can use for jerky is large. In fact, it's limited only by your imagination, interest, and willingness to experiment. Hunters typically have a wider range of animals to choose from because they are out in the wild. For those who don't hunt, the range of meats available is still extensive. Some wild and domestic meats that can be used include elk, moose, deer, cow, bison, antelope, rabbit, squirrel, sheep, goat, swine, and reindeer. Poultry and waterfowl, whether wild or domestic, can include chickens, turkeys, geese, ducks, and the ratites, ostrich and emu.

The most common variety of jerky—beef jerky—is easily sourced from a reputable butcher. Other meats at the butcher or a local quality supermarket should also be considered, such as chicken or turkey breasts and even ham. They can all be seasoned or flavored to suit your tastes. Of course, we'll also take a look at low-fat saltwater fish and freshwater fish. Fresh, frozen, or canned meats can be used, and even soybean products can be fashioned into jerky.

CUTTING WHOLE MEAT JERKY

Before we go through specific meat sources, let's address the three primary ways you'll slice and process meat to break it down into smaller, more manageable pieces. The most common way to do this for jerky is slicing into uniform strips, so we'll cover that first. Then we'll discuss the differences in technique used for making chunk and ground-meat jerkies. Keep in mind that you may develop techniques that work better for your particular situation or meat; these are only guidelines. Also, while the slicing information in particular was written particularly in regards to using beef, the most popular jerky meat, the basics can be used for many other animals including bison, chicken or other poultry, turkey, pig, sheep, lamb, and goat.

Before You Slice . . .

The meat cuts you select for jerky should be as lean as possible, meaning you will need to trim off as much fat as you can manage before proceeding to processing. Although fat adds flavor and juiciness to meat during a regular cooking process, it can be detrimental to jerky quality. The fat in meat can turn rancid and produce an off flavor if the meat is not eaten in a short time. This is one reason the top and bottom rounds of the hind quarters are often used for jerky making: they contain less fat. It is important to remove as much fat as possible if grinding the meat because the fat will become dispersed within the ground meat mixture. The less fat that is interspersed in ground meat, the better the jerky will dry.

Prior to cutting or slicing the meat, you should keep it very cold in your refrigerator or even just below freezing (30 degrees Fahrenheit). This will firm up the muscle and make it easier to slice, either by knife or with a slicer. If possible, use a mechanical slicer, as this will create more uniform pieces than using a knife. A steady hand with a sharp knife can suffice.

Buy as lean a cut of beef as possible for your jerky. Meat markets tend to leave some fat on the cut to add weight and enhance its appearance.

Begin by slicing off as much surface fat as possible. Fat will increase drying time for the meat and can cause off-flavors in storage if too much is dried along with the meat.

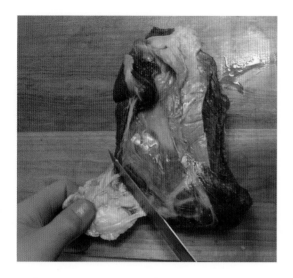

The silverskin that may cover some of the meat cut should be trimmed off. You can discard it as it has no nutritional value.

When you are finished trimming off the fat, the meat will be ready for slicing into strips.

Muscle fibers lay in bundles in various configurations, which gives them a striated appearance. These fibers form the basic mechanism that controls muscle contraction and movement. Skeletal muscles are most commonly used for jerky making. They are covered with a dense connective tissue sheath called the *epimysium*. Each of these muscles is divided into sections, called bundles, by a thick connective tissue layer called the *perimysium*. Clusters of fat cells, small blood vessels, and nerve bundles are found in this layer. The fat cells will appear white, most often as streaks through the meat or surrounding the bundles (what most people call marbling).

The muscle bundles lay in the same direction as they attach to the skeleton although some may overlap and attach in different areas of the same bone. The length of the muscle fibers will have striations, or grains, that appear in a horizontal position in relation to the bone. Cutting the muscle length-wise is referred to as cutting "with the grain." Cutting across the muscle is referred to as cutting "against the grain."

Slicing Strip Jerky

It is important to begin any cutting or slicing by using safe handling practices. Before the meat is taken from the refrigerator or freezer, clean all surfaces it will be exposed to. Wash your hands, knives, any mechanical slicer tray or blade, and all other surfaces the meat may come in contact with once is has been sliced, including meat trays. (Some slicers have trays attached alongside the blade to catch the meat slices as they are cut.) Be sure all parts of your slicer or your knife blade and handle have been thoroughly cleaned. Wash your cutting board or countertop and any bowls or utensils you will use with hot, soapy water, and then towel dry.

Whether using a mechanical slicer or knife, you can slice the meat either with the grain of the muscle fibers or against the grain. Slicing with the grain will give you slices that are easier to pull apart in strips because the tearing will follow the parallel meat fibers that lay lengthwise. Slicing the meat against the grain will produce a jerky that makes it somewhat easier to bite off a small

Using a mesh glove to firmly hold the meat while applying your knife can prevent accidental cuts to your hand.

Cutting with the grain of the meat will yield jerky that is easy to pull apart in strips.

Left: The muscle fiber direction will create striations. This will determine its grain when it's cut. Muscle fibers can run parallel in long lines or overlap to create cross fibers.

Above: Cutting against the grain of the meat will yield jerky that is easier to bite off in small pieces.

Your meat slices should be no thicker than ¼ inch. Strip width is not as much of a concern in the drying process as is thickness.

Keep a bowl of water available. Use it to dip your knife blade in periodically while slicing the meat. It will make the next cut easier.

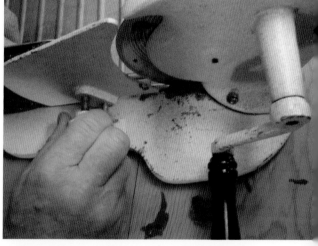

Left: A meat slicer can have three moving components: the blade, the handle to power it, and the meat tray, which moves back and forth.

Above: This hand slicer model has an adjustment knob on the side that allows you to increase or decrease the thickness of the meat slices.

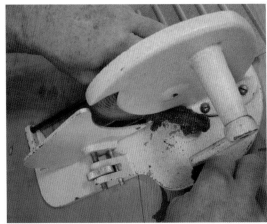

As the meat is sliced, it will separate and fall away from the blade.

Place the meat cut into the tray and press the plate firmly against it. At the same time you push the tray and meat forward toward the blade, turn the handle to rotate the blade and make your first slice.

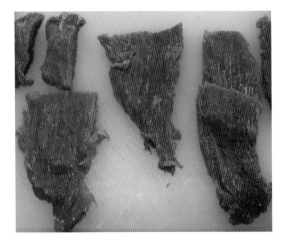

As each single piece is sliced, lay it aside to form rows in a clean pan or surface.

piece of the jerky strip without having to rip it with your teeth. The slicing direction is more of a personal choice.

The slices should be no more than ¼ inch in thickness but can be as long as the meat piece—as long as that length will fit in your dehydrator, of course. The thinner the strips are in thickness, the quicker they will dry.

If slicing with a knife, use a mesh glove on your free hand to avoid any injury from potential slippage of the blade. If you use a manual or electric mechanical slicer, the process will be much quicker than a knife. Most slicers have adjustment options to vary the thickness of the slices. They work well for most meats except fish and fowl because of their texture and size of portions available for slicing.

Slicing meat while it is still frozen or partially frozen makes it easier to produce uniform width pieces than soft meat. That is because raw meat will tend to squash as you cut into it, which makes it more difficult to cut consistent slices. Recipes for strip jerky begin on page 79.

Cutting Chunk Jerky

While slicing will result in flat strips of jerky that look like bacon, you can also cut small chunks or nuggets of meat to make into jerky. Cutting chunk jerky is easier than cutting slices, but thicker chunks require more drying time because of the denseness of the meat, and the interior of the meat must reach 160 degrees Fahrenheit. So time saved in one part of the process gets added in another. It really comes down to what you prefer to eat more than anything else.

One nice thing about chunk jerky is that you can use small or odd pieces of meat that are too small to be easily sliced into strips. This is often the case with upland game birds or waterfowl such as ducks and geese, and many small-game animals such as rabbits and squirrels. Recipes for chunk jerky are on pages 84 and 115.

Note: **One option would be to cut one larger piece to use for your test. If it has been heated through to 160 degrees Fahrenheit, you can be assured that all pieces smaller than it will have been as well.**

GROUND MEAT JERKY

Not all meat cut from a carcass will be the size you want for making jerky strips. Ground meat is a great way to use the scraps and small, oddly cut pieces made during the butchering process. Once ground, the meat can easily be formed into strips that are uniform in size and shape. There are other appeals to ground meat jerky as well. The resulting jerky is typically easier to chew than solid strips from one cut of meat. And some meats, such as the dark meat of ducks and geese, can be ground and mixed together with other meats with a milder flavor.

Chunk, cube, or nugget jerky can be made from meat pieces too small to slice.

Due to the nature of the jerky-making process, any meat processed with a hand or power grinder should be kept cold. Also, if you are making ground meat jerky and purchasing the meat from a grocery store or market, avoid buying meat that has already been ground. This will typically have fat added to it in the store's grinding process, partly as filler and partly as weight. Because the meat has now been processed and placed in a package or case, it has greater potential to be affected by *E. coli* and other bacteria. As mentioned previously, the more meat is processed and cut up, the more surface area is exposed to potential contamination. Grinding the meat yourself will ensure you have control over the entire process.

There are two basic types of grinders, electric and hand-powered, and depending on your preference, either will work. An electric model will generally provide great speed with its blade.

To slice meat for chunk jerky, begin with the smaller pieces. Slice them into about ¼- to ½-inch squares. Smaller meat pieces can also be ground up for ground meat jerky.

An old-fashioned hand grinder can be attached to a table or counter. Newer electric models may be easier for you to use. Place a clean dish under the blades to catch the ground-up meat.

Meat chunks or strips can be dropped into the top throat of the grinder. Be sure to keep your fingers away from the moving parts, and use extra care when using an electric model.

Use a meat rod to push the strips or chunks further into the grinder. Never use your fingers.

This can be both good and bad. Fast grinding speeds will process the meat more quickly but can also be a hazard if your fingers get too close. Some electric grinders may have speed settings that can increase or decrease the blade speed.

A hand-powered grinder's crank turns the internal worm gear to push the meat chunks into the cutting blade. These are slower than electric models and will require some physical effort. The more meat that is put into the chamber, the more resistance the crank will meet.

As with any jerky-making method, cleanliness and proper sanitation are key. Prior to using a hand-powered or electric grinder, disassemble all the parts possible and sterilize them in boiling water. Use this method of cleaning because the finer meat fibers and particles will be exposed to the inner surfaces of the grinder and plate. Sterilizing these surfaces before use will make sure there will be no contamination from the equipment. Be sure your electric grinder is not plugged in to an electrical outlet before you take it apart. Dry the parts and then put them back in place.

Note: **It might go without saying, but make sure there are no bones in the meat that could get mixed in during the grinding process. Bones may stop an electric grinder or damage the worm gear, grinding plate, and blade. Also, any bones that get ground up may cause problems like chipped teeth, and they increase the chance of your jerky harboring bacteria.**

It is more difficult to eliminate microorganisms that cause health problems in ground meat than with whole meat strips. It is vitally important that the oven, dehydrator, or smoker is capable of reaching temperatures of at least 200 degrees Fahrenheit. This is to ensure that an internal meat temperature of 160 degrees Fahrenheit can be achieved to destroy any disease-causing bacteria present.

If you use an oven to dry the meat, preheat it to 200 degrees Fahrenheit before placing the meat inside. If using racks, place metal sheets underneath to collect any drippings. Heat the meat for 1 to 2 hours with the door slightly open. Maintain the heat until the meat strips have been dried to the point where they bend but do not break when tested. It will be more difficult to determine the internal temperature of strips because of their thinness. You must test the pieces, however, to be sure it has reached a temperature of at least 160 degrees Fahrenheit.

Cutting the Meat

Let's go through the basic steps for grinding jerky.

1. Thoroughly wash your hands and any surface area that the meat may come into contact with before grinding. See pages 12, 14–16 for more on cleaning and sanitation.

2. Begin by cutting the meat into small chunks that will fit into the top opening of your grinder, sometimes referred to as the throat.

3. After cutting all the meat, lay the pieces out on a clean surface and sprinkle them with your seasonings (see pages 51–56 for recommendations). This will help mix them into the meat as it is being ground.

4. Grind the chunks slowly. Use a low-speed setting on your electric model and do not overload the grinder.

5. Let the meat fall into a clean container as it moves out of the grinding tube.

6. Use a clean meat stomper or plastic rod to gently push any wayward chunks into the grinder's throat. DO NOT push with your fingers. Always keep your fingers away from the moving parts. Using a rod to push the pieces into the grinder will also protect your meat from possible contamination from your hands.

7. Make sure you have clean hands before handling the meat. Put the ground meat into the refrigerator and cover it until you work with it again.

8. With the meat safely put away, you can unplug your grinder, disassemble the parts, and take your time cleaning it. Wash all the grinder parts in hot, soapy water and rinse with hot water. Make sure to clean the worm gear, too.

9. After allowing the parts to dry, store them in a cool, dry space until their next use. There are food-grade silicone sprays that you can apply to the parts to prevent rust. The spray will be washed off at the time of your next use.

Shaping the Meat

Shaping the pre-processed jerky meat is required more with ground jerky than with strips or chunks, which for the most part retain their shape. Because ground meat is a soft mass, it will be more difficult to form into strips—but it is not an impossible task.

Ground meat can be formed either into thin strips or fashioned into small pieces or nuggets. Make sure to thoroughly wash your hands before handling the meat. You can either use clean rubber gloves, thin clear plastic food-handling gloves, or roll the meat with very clean bare hands:

1. Mix the cure, seasonings, and flavorings of your choice thoroughly with the ground meat before molding it into the desired shape. See pages 45–49 for some recipes.

2. Begin forming the meat into strips by placing it on a sheet of food grade freezer paper or wax paper.

3. Place a second sheet of wax or freezer paper over the top. Use a rolling pin to roll the meat out into the form of a patty about ¼ inch thick.

4. Peel off the top paper and use a clean knife to slice the flat meat into strips about 1 inch wide. Make sure the knife isn't too sharp; you don't want to cut through the paper.

5. To avoid tearing the strips apart while transferring them to the jerky rack, flip the wax or freezer paper onto the rack. Then peel it off, leaving the strips behind.

Before you shape the ground meat, add your seasonings and cure, and mix in a nonmetallic bowl or container.

You should accurately measure out the ingredients you add to the meat, especially the cure mixture. Always pay attention to the package directions if using a commercial mix. Add the cure and seasonings to cold water.

Mix well.

Then pour over the ground meat and mix thoroughly.

Ground meat jerky can be shaped into thin jerky-style strips with the use of waxed paper or the waxed side of freezer paper.

Spread and hand-flatten a small ball of ground meat onto a sheet of waxed paper. Then place another sheet over the top.

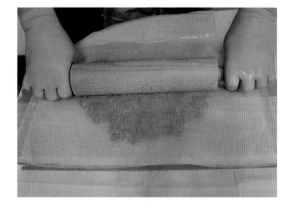

Use a rolling pin to roll the meat out flat to between a ⅛- and ¼-inch thickness.

Peel off the top sheet of waxed paper.

Use a clean table knife, without a sharp edge, to cut the meat into long, even strips.

Place your oven rack or dehydrator tray on top of the meat. Then lift the waxed paper with the cut strips on it and the rack together and flip everything over so the waxed paper is now on top. Peel off the paper.

6. Dry until an internal temperature reaches 160 degrees Fahrenheit to eliminate any disease-causing bacteria. Drying in an oven at a setting of 200 to 275 degrees Fahrenheit should help you attain the required internal temperature in one to two hours.

If you find this method isn't for you, you can also try partially freezing the ground meat on plastic wrap by first flattening it out in a ¼-inch-thick layer and putting it in the freezer. After hardening enough to handle easily but before completely frozen, cut it into strips. Peel off the plastic wrap and lay the pieces on the drying rack.

The strips are now ready for drying. Make sure there is no meat overlapping onto another piece.

Using Extruders

A meat extruder is a piece of equipment used to form meat into certain shapes, often flat or round, with an interchangeable tip. It resembles a caulk gun or a cookie-making gun. In this case, meat is packed into a hollow tube and pressure is applied against the meat by squeezing the handles together. This pressure then pushes an interior plate forward, and the meat is pushed out the opposite end in the shape formed by the tip.

Any leftover ground meat can be shaped into sticks by hand and put into an extruder gun. A second method of using leftover meat is to form it into a 1-inch-thick block or slab, wrap it in plastic, and then freeze it. Then remove the wrap and slice into ¼-inch-thick strips.

While hand-held extruder models are easy to use, they may take some hand and arm strength to squeeze the handle, particularly at the start when the tube is completely full of meat. If that's a concern, you may consider buying a grinder that has an attachment for making meat strips or round sticks.

Here are the steps for using a hand extruder:

1. Make sure that all parts of a handheld extruder or a grinder-extruder model have been disassembled prior to use and thoroughly cleaned and dried. Wash your hands thoroughly before handling the meat.

2. To begin, wet your hands or gloves in cold water before scooping a cup of the cured and seasoned meat and placing it on a clean surface.

3. Pick up a portion of the meat and roll it between your hands to form it into a cylindrical shape that is small enough to slide into the tube. Then add more small rolls until the tube is full. The meat will flow out more easily if it has been formed into thin rolls first rather than packing the tube full.

4. Place the plunger into the tube and secure the molding tip at the opposite end. Refer to the instructions that came with the extruder if necessary.

5. Spray your dehydrator tray, oven, or smoker rack with vegetable oil so the meat will not stick. Gently squeeze the handles of the extruder together and extrude the strips or sticks onto the tray or rack. Squeeze until the desired length is reached.

6. Once the tube is empty, you can remove the plunger and refill the tube.

7. Repeat the extruding steps until all of the meat you have prepared is used up. You are now ready to dry the jerky.

8. Thoroughly clean the tube, plunger, nozzle tips, and anything else used with hot, soapy water.

Note: Mix only the meat you can process at one time, and use it as soon as it's mixed. Do not store meat in tubes or nozzle tips overnight as it will be very difficult to push out after it has cooled to refrigerator temperatures.

Fashion the ground meat into small sticks by rolling a handful between your fingers or hands. Wet your hands or gloves with cold water to keep the meat from sticking.

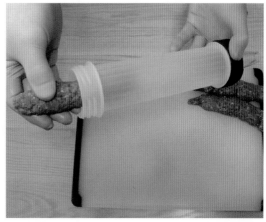

Slide the meat rolls into the extruder tube and reassemble the handle and plunger.

Gently squeeze the handle to push the ground meat out the tip and onto a rack or screen. The resulting extruded ground-meat jerky is ready to place in the dehydrator or oven.

Space the ground meat jerky in the dehydrator to encourage even airflow. You may want to rotate the racks from top to bottom during the drying process.

Ground meat jerky will have an elongated shape if you use an extruder. Whether strips or sticks, allow them to cool in the refrigerator after you remove them from the dehydrator.

GROUND TERIYAKI JERKY

1 POUND GROUND MEAT

MARINADE

½ cup teriyaki sauce

1 tablespoon olive oil

1 teaspoon garlic, minced

1 teaspoon salt

1 teaspoon ground black pepper

¼ teaspoon liquid smoke

In a nonmetallic container, thoroughly mix the teriyaki sauce, olive oil, minced garlic, salt, black pepper, and liquid smoke. Allow the flavors to blend for 15 minutes. Add the ground meat and mix thoroughly. Cover the container and marinate for 1 hour in the refrigerator, or leave overnight if more marinating time is desired. Remove from the marinade container and form into shapes as outlined on pages 40–44. Using one of the four methods described in Chapter 3 (starting on page 58), dry the meat. Make sure the meat reaches an internal temperature of 165°F rather than the standard 160°F. Check the jerky's progress after 4 hours and continue drying as needed. Keep in mind that the thicker the strips, the longer it will take. Once your jerky is done, let it cool, and then store it in sealed jars in the refrigerator.

GROUND SOY JERKY

1 POUND GROUND MEAT

MARINADE

½ cup soy sauce

1 tablespoon vegetable oil

1 tablespoon light brown sugar

1 teaspoon garlic, minced

½ teaspoon ground ginger

½ teaspoon ground black pepper

In a nonmetallic container, thoroughly mix the soy sauce, oil, sugar, garlic, ginger, and black pepper. Allow the flavors to blend for 15 minutes. Add the ground meat and mix thoroughly. Cover the container and marinate for 1 hour in the refrigerator, or leave overnight if more marinating time is desired. Remove from the marinade container and form into shapes as outlined on pages 40–44. Using one of the four methods described in Chapter 3 (starting on page 58), dry the meat. Make sure the meat reaches an internal temperature of 165°F rather than the standard 160°F. Check the jerky's progress after 4 hours and continue drying as needed. Keep in mind that the thicker the strips, the longer it will take. Once your jerky is done, let it cool, and then store it in sealed jars in the refrigerator.

TOMATO SOY JERKY

1 POUND GROUND MEAT

MARINADE

½ cup tomato sauce

3 tablespoons soy sauce

2 tablespoons Worcestershire sauce

1 tablespoon white wine vinegar

1 tablespoon light brown sugar

1 teaspoon onion, finely chopped

1 teaspoon salt

1 teaspoon garlic powder

1 teaspoon ground black pepper

1 teaspoon horseradish

½ teaspoon Tabasco sauce

½ teaspoon liquid smoke

In a nonmetallic container, mix the tomato sauce, soy sauce, Worcestershire sauce, vinegar, sugar, onion, salt, garlic powder, pepper, horseradish, Tabasco sauce, and liquid smoke. Allow the flavors to blend for 15 minutes. Add the ground meat and mix thoroughly. Cover the container and marinate for 1 hour in the refrigerator, or leave overnight if more marinating time is desired. Remove from the marinade container and form into shapes as outlined on pages 40–44. Using one of the four methods in Chapter 3 (starting on page 58), dry the meat. Make sure the meat reaches an internal temperature of 165°F rather than the standard 160°F. Check the jerky's progress after 4 hours and continue drying as needed. Keep in mind that the thicker the strips, the longer it will take. Once your jerky is done, let it cool, and then store it in sealed jars in the refrigerator.

BEER CHEESE JERKY

1 POUND GROUND MEAT

MARINADE

½ cup beer

1 cup grated Parmesan cheese

2 tablespoons soy sauce

1 tablespoon vegetable oil

1 teaspoon garlic, minced

1 teaspoon dried basil

½ teaspoon salt

½ teaspoon ground black pepper

½ teaspoon liquid smoke

Mix the beer and Parmesan cheese together in a small bowl. In a nonmetallic container, mix the soy sauce, oil, garlic, basil, salt, pepper, and liquid smoke. Add the beer and cheese mixture. Allow the flavors to blend for 15 minutes. Add the ground meat and mix thoroughly. Cover the container and marinate for 1 hour in the refrigerator, or leave overnight if more marinating time is desired. Remove from the marinade container and form into shapes as outlined on pages 40–44. Using one of the four methods in Chapter 3 (starting on page 58), dry the meat. Make sure the meat reaches an internal temperature of 165°F rather than the standard 160°F. Check the jerky's progress after 4 hours and continue drying as needed. Keep in mind that the thicker the strips, the longer it will take. Once your jerky is done, let it cool, and then store it in sealed jars in the refrigerator.

ROSEMARY WINE JERKY

1 POUND GROUND MEAT

MARINADE

½ cup dry white wine

1 tablespoon olive oil

1 tablespoon lemon juice

1 tablespoon Worcestershire sauce

1 tablespoon onion, minced

1 tablespoon honey

1 teaspoon salt

1 teaspoon dried basil

1 teaspoon dried oregano

1 teaspoon garlic, minced

1 teaspoon ground black pepper

1 teaspoon dried rosemary, crushed

In a nonmetallic container, thoroughly mix the wine, oil, lemon juice, Worcestershire sauce, onion, honey, salt, basil, oregano, garlic, pepper, and rosemary together. Allow the flavors to blend for 15 minutes. Add the ground meat and mix thoroughly. Cover the container and marinate for 1 hour in the refrigerator, or leave overnight if more marinating time is desired. Remove from the marinade container and form into shapes as outlined on pages 40–44. Using one of the four methods in Chapter 3 (starting on page 58), dry the meat. Make sure the meat reaches an internal temperature of 165°F rather than the standard 160°F. Check the jerky's progress after 4 hours and continue drying as needed. Keep in mind that the thicker the strips, the longer it will take. Once your jerky is done, let it cool, and then store it in sealed jars in the refrigerator.

TOMATO VODKA JERKY

1 POUND GROUND MEAT

MARINADE

½ cup vodka

¼ cup tomato juice

¼ cup Worcestershire sauce

1 teaspoon sugar

1 teaspoon celery salt

½ teaspoon Tabasco sauce

¼ teaspoon horseradish

¼ teaspoon ground black pepper

⅛ teaspoon lemon juice

¼ teaspoon liquid smoke

In a nonmetallic container, thoroughly mix the vodka, tomato juice, Worcestershire sauce, sugar, celery salt, Tabasco sauce, horseradish, pepper, lemon juice, and liquid smoke. Allow the flavors to blend for 15 minutes. Add the ground meat and mix thoroughly. Cover the container and marinate for 1 hour in the refrigerator, or leave overnight if more marinating time is desired. Remove from the marinade container and form into shapes as outlined on pages 40–44. Using one of the four methods in Chapter 3 (starting on page 58), dry the meat. Make sure the meat reaches an internal temperature of 165°F rather than the standard 160°F. Check the jerky's progress after 4 hours and continue drying as needed. Keep in mind that the thicker the strips, the longer it will take. Once your jerky is done, let it cool, and then store it in sealed jars in the refrigerator.

RED WINE JERKY

1 POUND GROUND MEAT

MARINADE

1 cup red wine

½ cup onion, chopped

1 tablespoon olive oil

2 teaspoons light brown sugar

1 teaspoon salt

1 tablespoon chopped fresh basil

1 teaspoon garlic, minced

½ teaspoon ground black pepper

½ teaspoon liquid smoke

In a saucepan over medium heat, reduce the wine to ½ cup. In a skillet, sauté the onion in olive oil over medium heat until lightly browned. Add the reduced wine and allow it to heat until it just begins to boil. Remove the skillet from heat. Add the sugar, salt, basil, garlic, pepper, and liquid smoke. Allow the flavors to blend for 15 minutes. Allow to cool slightly, then pour into blender. Blend. Place the meat in a nonmetallic container, add the blended marinade, and mix thoroughly. Cover the container and marinate for 1 hour in the refrigerator, or leave overnight if more marinating time is desired. Remove from marinade container and form into shapes as outlined on pages 40–44. Using one of the four methods in Chapter 3 (starting on page 58), dry the meat. Make sure the meat reaches an internal temperature of 165°F rather than the standard 160°F. Check the jerky's progress after 4 hours and continue drying as needed. Keep in mind that the thicker the strips, the longer it will take. Once your jerky is done, let it cool, and then store it in sealed jars in the refrigerator.

MEXICAN TACO JERKY

1 POUND GROUND MEAT

MARINADE

1½ ounces taco mix

½ cup salsa

¼ cup fresh non-chlorinated water

1 teaspoon salt

½ teaspoon liquid smoke

In a nonmetallic container, mix taco mix, salsa, water, salt, and liquid smoke thoroughly until the dry ingredients are dissolved. Place in a blender and puree. Allow the flavors to blend for 15 minutes. Add the ground meat and mix thoroughly. Cover the container and marinate for 1 hour in the refrigerator, or leave overnight if more marinating time is desired. Remove from the marinade container and form into shapes as outlined on pages 40–44. Using one of the four methods in Chapter 3 (starting on page 58), dry the meat. Make sure the meat reaches an internal temperature of 165°F rather than the standard 160°F. Check the jerky's progress after 4 hours and continue drying as needed. Keep in mind that the thicker the strips, the longer it will take. Once your jerky is done, let it cool, and then store it in sealed jars in the refrigerator.

GROUND TURKEY JERKY

1 POUND GROUND TURKEY

MARINADE

2 tablespoons lemon juice

2 tablespoons onion, minced

2 tablespoons teriyaki sauce

1 tablespoon sugar

1 tablespoon olive oil

2 teaspoons paprika

1 teaspoon minced garlic

1 teaspoon salt

1 teaspoon ground black pepper

¼ teaspoon Tabasco sauce

½ teaspoon liquid smoke

In a nonmetallic container, thoroughly mix the lemon juice, onion, teriyaki sauce, sugar, oil, paprika, garlic, salt, pepper, Tabasco sauce, and liquid smoke. Allow the flavors to blend for 15 minutes. Add the ground meat and mix thoroughly. Cover the container and marinate for 1 hour in the refrigerator, or leave overnight if more marinating time is desired. Remove from the marinade container and form into shapes as outlined on pages 40–44. Using one of the four methods in Chapter 3 (starting on page 58), dry the meat. Make sure the meat reaches an internal temperature of 165°F rather than the standard 160°F. Check the jerky's progress after 4 hours and continue drying as needed. Keep in mind that the thicker the strips, the longer it will take. Once your jerky is done, let it cool, and then store it in sealed jars in the refrigerator.

ONION JERKY

1 POUND GROUND MEAT

MARINADE

2 cups finely chopped onion

2 tablespoons light brown sugar

2 tablespoons teriyaki sauce

1 teaspoon olive oil

1 teaspoon garlic, minced

1 teaspoon salt

¼ cup raw onion, minced

¼ teaspoon ground black pepper

Place 2 cups finely chopped onions in a sauté pan over low heat. Add the brown sugar when partially cooked and continue to stir and cook until caramelized and completely soft. Do not burn. Remove from heat. In a nonmetallic container, thoroughly mix the teriyaki sauce, olive oil, garlic, salt, raw minced onion, and black pepper. Add to caramelized onion. Allow the flavors to blend for 15 minutes. Add the ground meat and mix thoroughly. Cover the container and marinate for 1 hour in the refrigerator, or leave overnight if more marinating time is desired. Remove from the marinade container and form into shapes as outlined on pages 40–44. Using one of the four methods in Chapter 3 (starting on page 58), dry the meat. Make sure the meat reaches an internal temperature of 165°F rather than the standard 160°F. Check the jerky's progress after 4 hours and continue drying as needed. Keep in mind that the thicker the strips, the longer it will take. Once your jerky is done, let it cool, and then store it in sealed jars in the refrigerator.

CURING AND MARINADES

Curing meat is one of the oldest preservation methods used by humans, and it's still one of the most useful preservation methods available. Through the millennia, salt was the primary preservative used for meat and fish as civilizations strove to create a longer "shelf life" for meat products. You'll notice that the modern methods for curing still give the meat a salty character thanks not only salt but also nitrite—both of which are used to prevent botulism from growing. Luckily, many people enjoy the salty flavor of cured meats!

The term *cure* is sometimes interpreted to mean both curing and the subsequent smoking of meat. However, curing does not actually imply smoking, although the two processes work together well. Strictly speaking, curing applies only to dry salt curing, brine submersion, or pickling with a vinegar base. In a wider sense, however, curing applies to any saline or alkaline preservation solution, perhaps with some modifications.

***Note:* "Cure" can be used to describe either the actual process of turning raw meat into a preserved, safe, and edible meat or the commercial product pack, which contains the essential ingredients that creates the transformation.**

Curing is generally done using either a liquid marinade into which the meat is submerged or a dry rub, which is used to coat the meat's exterior. Typically, the meat must sit for a certain length of time before drying in order for the cure to work through the exterior meat surface and into the interior. This is accomplished by osmosis as the salt slowly moves through the cell membranes. Generally speaking, the larger the piece of meat being cured, the longer it will take to complete the curing process.

Marinating meat or vegetables involves soaking foods in a usually acidic liquid that often contains flavorings, seasonings, and salts.

Cures and seasonings add flavor to the jerky and help with preservation. These can be added to the ground meat before shaping. Be sure to thoroughly mix the cure and seasonings with the meat.

Depending on the food used and personal preferences, this process may last several minutes, hours, or days.

The acids in marinades help to break down the surface tissues, which some advocates believe allows more of the seasoned liquids to be absorbed inside, resulting in a more flavorful product. Marinades, however, react more to the surface of the meat rather than penetrating inside. Meat protein contains about 75 percent water and thus has little room to absorb more moisture.

Marinating is not tenderizing, which is a process that causes proteins in meat to soften and make it more tender to the chew. A good marinade must balance the acid, oil, and spice in order for the meat to not become too acidic, which can produce harsh or off flavors.

Always marinate meat in your refrigerator. Never marinate at room temperature, because this will put the meat in dangerous temperatures where bacteria multiplies quickly (the danger zone is between 40 and 140 degrees Fahrenheit). Never use a recipe that calls for marinating at room temperature.

The drying time is not significantly affected by marinating the meat. The temperature at which the meat is dried is more important than the length of time spent drying, although these two dynamics have required levels to produce a safe product (more on this on page 62).

Ground meat used for jerky making is typically not placed in a marinade because it can become too soft and unmanageable when formed into strips or sticks. Liquids in small amounts and dry ingredients can be successfully mixed into ground meat without it losing the firm consistency necessary for handling.

Salt

Salt is the essential ingredient in the curing process. It draws moisture and blood from the muscle cells while entering the cells by osmosis. This process distributes the salt through the tissue and induces partial drying. Salt also inhibits the action and function of certain bacteria and enzymes.

This is why salt is one of the most common ingredients used in the production of jerky. It is central to all curing mixtures. Salt is hygroscopic, which means it absorbs moisture from its surrounding environment. This is its preservative action.

Choose a good-quality, food-grade salt for your curing process, such as a coarse pickling or canning salt. These readily dissolve in liquids, which make them easy to use. Using a non-iodized salt in a marinade or brine is also best as it prevents potential chemical reactions if you're using heat.

Salt makes up the bulk of any curing mixture not only because it is a good preservative: it also provides a desirable flavor. Curing salt (sodium nitrite) can be used in homemade jerky, although it is not required. Commercial cures are readily available. These typically contain some form of salt as the main preserving agent but can also contain sugar, sodium nitrate, sodium nitrite, and propylene glycol (which helps to keep the mixture uniform).

There are also store-bought mixes available that contain all ingredients and spices in one packet, such as Morton Tender Quick, Hi Mountain Jerky Cure and Seasoning, Presto Seasonings, and Nesco. Using these will help speed up your jerky production. These mixes can serve as a base for exploring your own variations as long as the rates and ratios used coincide with the amount of meat being used.

Failing to maintain the proper level of curing ingredients in relation to the meat weight volume will lead to underprocessing. The sugar or pepper levels, for instance, can be increased to make a sweeter or more flavorful final product, but neither will affect the curing of the jerky.

If you use a commercial cure mix, follow the directions exactly regarding the amounts and mixing procedure. If you create your own cure, be sure to use precise amounts of all ingredients called for in your cure recipe and calculate precisely.

Curing can be accomplished by using one of two methods: marinating the meat in liquid or coating it with a dry rub. Typically, the meat must be in contact with the marinade or rub a length of time before drying in order for the cure to work through the muscle fibers.

Sodium Nitrate and Sodium Nitrite

Nitrates and nitrites are chemical compounds that contain nitrogen and oxygen and are commonly used in curing meat. They have been used in place of salt for many years and are typically added in the first step of any commercially cured product to inhibit bacterial growth. Their action removes the moisture that bacteria could live on and kill the bacteria through dehydration. Sodium nitrate is particularly effective in food preservation and is widely used because it allows the food to last longer.

Many family recipes handed down through the generations used saltpeter, or potassium nitrate, for curing. Most meat supply companies no longer sell saltpeter, but you may find other commercial products that will achieve similar results. There are commercial fast-cures available that contain 0.5 percent sodium nitrate and 0.5 percent sodium nitrite. If used, they are typically found in recipes at a ratio of 1 teaspoon (0.17 ounces or 7 grams) per 1 pound of meat.

You should be aware of the health concerns that sodium nitrate and sodium nitrite have posed for many people. At too high of a level, they can be detrimental to health.

Sensitivities to nitrates and nitrites can cause migraine headaches or allergic reactions for some people. At high enough levels, these compounds can be carcinogenic, and a single dose, if large enough, can be lethal. A fatal dose of potassium nitrate for an adult is 30 to 35 grams ingested in a single sitting. Sodium nitrite is lethal at about 22 milligrams per kilogram of adult body weight, or about the same amount as potassium nitrate. To reach a lethal toxicity level, an adult weighing 150 pounds would have to consume about 20 pounds of brine-cured meat containing 200 parts per million (ppm) nitrite in one meal. It goes without saying that it would take extraordinary stamina to eat enough to reach that lethal level. (Even if a person could eat that amount of meat in one sitting, it is likely that the salt level, not the nitrite, would create the toxicity.) Keep in mind that the normal American diet contains more nitrates from leafy vegetables such as celery, spinach, radishes, cabbage, beets, and lettuce than from cured meats because these plants readily absorb nitrogen fertilizers used in food production.

Note: **Two hundred ppm is designated as a "safe" level of nitrates or nitrites by the USDA. This figure represents the grams of nitrate and nitrite times one million divided by the grams of cured meat that it treats. For example, 200 ppm of nitrate for 50 grams of cured meat is equal to 0.01 grams of nitrate (0.01 x 1 million ÷ 50 = 200 ppm). This level preserves the antimicrobial power of these compounds while preventing the development of carcinogenic concentrations. It is difficult to remove nitrates or nitrites from the meat-curing process without increasing the risk of harmful bacteria, particularly botulism.**

Marinades

Marinades are liquid brines or pickles in which meat or fish are soaked to enrich flavor prior to drying. A wide range of flavors can be created and may only be limited by your imagination. Some ingredients in marinades, such as salt and sodium nitrate, cure the meat and help preserve it. Other ingredients, such as vinegar and soy sauce, will help enhance the flavor, texture, and even appearance of the meat. Generally speaking, the amount of marinade needed is dependent upon the amount of meat being processed. If you are allowing the meat to marinate overnight, make sure all pieces are completely submerged in the liquid. On the other hand, you will need less marinade if you are just dipping the meat pieces into it and then laying them on a rack. Recipes throughout this book use marinades, but the following three marinades will give you an idea of typical combinations of ingredients for 2 pounds of meat.

A liquid marinade is often used for jerky. Thoroughly mix all ingredients in a nonmetallic container.

LEMON-GARLIC MARINADE

½ cup lemon juice

½ cup olive or vegetable oil

2 teaspoons dried oregano leaves

1 teaspoon prepared yellow mustard

3 cloves garlic, minced

⅛ teaspoon ground black pepper

Combine the lemon juice, oil, oregano, mustard, garlic, and pepper in a small saucepan and heat until bubbly, stirring constantly. Remove from heat and let cool to room temperature before use.

Submerge the meat strips into the marinade until both sides are completely covered. Cover the container and let it sit in your refrigerator for 8 to 10 hours, or overnight.

ASIAN MARINADE

¼ cup sliced green onions

3 teaspoons soy sauce

2 teaspoons honey

1 teaspoon sesame oil

1 teaspoon molasses

Combine the onions, soy sauce, honey, oil, and molasses in a small saucepan and stir well. Heat until warm but not bubbly. Remove from heat and let cool to room temperature before use.

GREEK MARINADE

½ cup olive oil

½ cup sweet vermouth

1 teaspoon lemon juice

¾ teaspoon dried tarragon leaves

1 small red onion, thinly sliced

⅛ teaspoon ground black pepper

Combine the oil, vermouth, lemon juice, tarragon, onion, and pepper in a small saucepan and heat until bubbly, stirring constantly. Remove from heat and let cool to room temperature before use.

Dry Rub Cures

A dry rub cure consists of a mix of dry ingredients including common salt and other preservatives, as found in commercial cures (see page 51), that is sprinkled on and then rubbed into the meat. The ingredients are then allowed to work into the meat before it is dried. Dry cures typically contain herbs and spices, and some contain sugar or other sweeteners.

If you are using a dry rub, it is best to allow 24 hours for it to work into the meat. This will require that it be put in a pan, covered, and left in your refrigerator until ready for use. A basic recipe for a dry rub cure for about 2 pounds of meat might look like this:

CLASSIC DRY RUB

2 teaspoons salt

1 teaspoon ground black pepper

1 teaspoon garlic powder

½ teaspoon ground white pepper

1 tablespoon light brown sugar

1 package commercial cure product

Combine the ingredients in a bowl. Coat the meat slices with the rub on both sides. Cover and refrigerate for 24 hours before drying.

A dry rub cure can be sprinkled or rubbed onto the jerky meat. Mix the ingredients thoroughly before applying them to the meat.

If you sprinkle a cure on the meat, use a sugar shaker that has large holes.

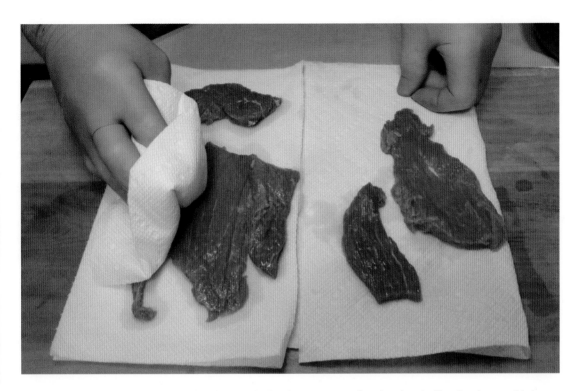

Once you've marinated the strips, remove them from the marinade, place them on paper towels, and pat them dry. Then place them on a dehydrator tray or oven rack for drying.

Flavorings

Depending on your tastes, there are several flavoring agents that can be used when curing jerky, including herbs and spices, sugar, liquid smoke, and oil.

Herbs and spices: Whether added whole, crushed, ground, pureed, fresh, or dried, there are many herbs and spices that can be used to add flavors in jerky. You can include such herbs as basil, oregano, sage, mint, dill, rosemary, thyme, chives, parsley, or savory. Spices such as cayenne, chili powder, curry, garlic, ginger, allspice, mustard, nutmeg, and horseradish are only a few that are available, depending on your tastes. One of the most common spices used

in jerky making is pepper. Black pepper is most used because it adds flavor and color.

Sugar: Sugar is an important ingredient because it helps moderate the intensity of the salt flavor. This moderating effect helps reduce the perception of saltiness.

Liquid smoke: Liquid smoke is a popular flavoring for jerky. However, if too much is added, it can overpower the meat flavor and even create a harsh, bitter flavor: this is an instance when using more is not better. Liquid smoke is derived from burning sawdust, condensing the smoke, and separating out the carcinogenic compounds

For a dry rub, first thoroughly mix all ingredients. Then place the meat strips in a nonmetallic container and sprinkle the dry rub on the top of the meat.

Next, roll the meat strips in the dry rub.

Coat all sides thoroughly. For most cure and seasoning mixes to be used properly and safely, you must know the exact amount of meat being used.

such as tar, resin, and soot. It most often can be found in mesquite or hickory flavors. Liquid smoke is safer to use than using real smoke, such as in a smoke house or wood smoker. The intensity of the smoke flavor often depends on the amount used. Liquid smoke can be used with food dehydrators and is the only way to add a smoky flavor in a dehydrator.

Oils: Some oils used in jerky making include those derived from olives, sesame seeds, and basil. Oils can add flavor but will not dry on the jerky. They can help add texture but will need to be patted off the jerky with paper towels during the drying process.

Other ingredients: Marinades can also include onions, fruits, or vegetables. Juices from lemons, oranges, apples, or tomatoes can be used, too, along with various kinds of peppers. Crushing, mincing, and mashing these ingredients will create more surface area to transfer their flavor to the liquid.

Place the rubbed strips in a glass or plastic container or in a resealable plastic bag to cure.

Different marinades can be used with ground meat jerky. Thoroughly mix the ingredients in a nonmetallic container.

Mix the ground meat and marinade thoroughly before fashioning into strips.

Then pour evenly over the ground meat.

These pieces of ground meat bison jerky have been infused with cranberries and black pepper.

Chapter 3
MAKING JERKY

Making jerky is relatively simple and can be done by anyone who has access to a kitchen and a dehydrator or smoker. You don't need any special expertise, but you do need to understand and follow some easy directions. Like homebrewing or canning, making jerky at home requires attention to a few basic principles to ensure a safe, stable food product.

Making your own jerky allows you to choose from a wide variety of meats, such as beef, chicken, fish, wild game, and waterfowl. It also puts you in control of the kind and intensity of flavors in your jerky, and it allows you to create a high-quality product without chemical stabilizers or preservatives. This chapter will walk you through the steps required to produce safe, top-quality jerky and will discuss some of the equipment you'll use.

FOUR WAYS TO MAKE JERKY

Given sufficiently low humidity and enough sun, thin slices of meat will dry in the open air. While this primitive method may have worked for Native Americans and pioneers, it is not recommended today because it can foster bacterial growth and expose the meat to insect or animal contamination and spoilage. Instead, you will need to use a dehydrator or a smoker, sometimes in combination with an oven. The equipment you use does not need to be expensive or fancy, but it must be reliable, especially with respect to temperature control.

It was long believed that meats for jerky only needed to reach 145 degrees Fahrenheit to ensure the safety of the finished product. Some years ago, however, several incidents of food-borne illnesses linked to commercial and homemade jerky spurred research by food scientists into the processes needed to inactivate bacterial pathogens in the meat. As a result of that research, the USDA now recommends that to make jerky safely you should heat the meat to an internal temperature of 160 degrees Fahrenheit (poultry to 165 degrees) before drying. Fish can still be heated to 145 degrees and be used safely.

In this book, we'll focus on four ways to make jerky:

1. High-Temperature Dehydrator (page 65)

2. Oven and Low-Temperature Dehydrator (page 67)

3. Smoker and Low-Temperature Dehydrator (page 72)

4. Smoker (page 73)

Dehydrators

There are two main types of home dehydrators available today. The first is the stacking dehydrator. Sometimes called "round" dehydrators (although some are actually rectangular in shape), the stacking dehydrator is composed of an electrical

Your home oven can be used together with a dehydrator to safely make jerky. See page 67 for instructions.

Jerky strips can be suspended from oven racks for drying. Use a toothpick and slip it through the top of each strip and position them on the racks so they do not touch each other. Be sure to cover the bottom of the oven with tin foil before preheating it and adding the meat. The foil will catch the drippings as the meat is drying.

heating element and a fan, which are located either at the top or the base of the unit, and which work together to circulate heated air around vertically stacked trays of food. The trays are usually perforated with a large hole in the center of each tray to enable the heated air to circulate properly through the stacked trays. The warm air circulating around the trays dries the food. Stacking dehydrators tend to be fairly compact and relatively inexpensive, and some models allow their owners to expand drying capacity simply by adding additional trays that can be purchased from the manufacturer.

To release some of the moisture from the oven, use a wooden spoon to crack the door. Continue to monitor the temperature during the drying process so the appropriate temperature is maintained. Do not leave it unattended.

The main disadvantage of most stacking dehydrators is inherent to their design. As the heated air moves through the multiple trays of food, it cools, so food in the trays farthest from the heating element dries more slowly than food in the trays closer to the heat source. The trays need to be rotated during the drying process to get all the food to dehydrate at roughly the same rate, and the more trays you have, the more diligently you have to rotate them. It's noteworthy that some popular Nesco stacking dehydrators solve this problem with a technology that pushes the heated air through an exterior pressure chamber and then horizontally across the food, substantially reducing the need to rotate trays.

Stacking dehydrators that have the heating element and fan at the bottom of the appliance are often the least expensive dehydrators. If moisture and crumbs fall from the trays into the heating element and fan, however, these dehydrators can be hard to clean—and their durability may suffer.

Some popular models of stacking dehydrators are the Nesco FD-80A, the Waring Pro, the Presto 06301, the L'Equip 528, and the Nesco Snackmaster Pro.

Avoid using a dehydrator that has an exposed heat coil at its base. Any fat from drying meats

Insulated variable-temperature smokers can provide reliable temperature control while taking up little space.

that drips onto this coil can create a fire hazard. If yours has one, be sure to cover the coils with aluminum foil so any drippings don't reach the coils.

The second type of home dehydrator is the side-fan dehydrator, sometimes called a "square" dehydrator. These have a heating element and a fan mounted on the back side of the device, blowing warm air across multiple trays that are made to slide in and out of a door on the opposite side of the unit. This arrangement helps ensure fast and even drying of the food, as well as the durability of the appliance. And it's easy to check the progress of the drying process, which can be troublesome with a stacking dehydrator, which requires that you unstack the trays to see the food inside. Side-fan dehydrators, however, are generally more expensive than stacking dehydrators, and they take up more counter space. Also, the capacity of a side-fan dehydrator can't be increased by adding additional trays. Raw-food enthusiasts and others who use their dehydrators frequently often prefer side-fan models. Some popular side-fan dehydrators include the Excalibur 3500B and 3926TB.

Note: There are a few dehydrators that have no fan, but instead rely entirely on convection to heat and dry the food. They're quiet and do a good job on some kinds of foods, but much longer drying times makes them less than ideal for making jerky.

Both kinds of dehydrators can be used for making jerky, but the process you'll use depends on a key variable: the temperature that can be reached by your dehydrator. Many inexpensive dehydrators have only one temperature setting, which is set by the manufacturer. Designed primarily for drying fruits, nuts, and vegetables, these dehydrators usually will heat to around 140 degrees Fahrenheit, which isn't high enough to ensure food safety in meat jerky. If you have one of these single-setting dehydrators or a variable-temperature model that won't reach 160 degrees Fahrenheit, you'll need to precook the meat to an internal temperature of 160 degrees Fahrenheit (165 degrees for poultry) before putting it in your dehydrator to dry. For our purposes, any dehydrator that can reach 160 degrees Fahrenheit (or 165 degrees if you intend to make poultry jerky) is a "high-temperature" dehydrator, while dehydrators that won't reach that temperature are "low-temperature" dehydrators.

So, before drying meat in a low-temperature dehydrator, you will first cook it in your oven to an internal temperature of 160 degrees Fahrenheit (165 degrees for poultry). After heating your meat to 160 degrees Fahrenheit, you'll move it to your dehydrator and maintain a constant dehydration temperature of 130 to 140 degrees Fahrenheit for 4 to 6 hours or until it's done. This is important because the process must be fast enough to dry food before it spoils, and it must remove enough water to prevent microorganisms from flourishing. If the proper temperature is maintained, this two-step process will yield a safe finished product. Of course, if you have a high-temperature dehydrator that will heat the food to 160 degrees Fahrenheit (or 165 degrees for poultry), you don't have to precook your jerky in the oven.

Note: Fats and oils typically do not dry. This is due to their composition and the melting points needed to disperse their molecules. This is one reason for cutting off or trimming as much fat as possible when you are preparing meat and fish for making jerky: it reduces the likelihood that fat will become rancid and spoil your jerky after drying. In wild game, removing fat also helps reduce the gamey flavor. If using fatty meats in a dehydrator or oven, use a

paper towel to pat off any fat beads that form on the meat strips during the heating process.

Meat jerky made in a high-temperature dehydrator is a little different from that made by the two-step oven-and-dehydrator process. Jerky that's first cooked in the oven tends to be a little lighter in color and a little more tender than jerky prepared entirely in a high-temperature dehydrator. Some people prefer the jerky made by the two-step process, but jerky dried entirely in a high-temperature dehydrator looks and tastes more like what most people think of as traditional jerky.

Depending on a number of variables, such as meat thickness, amount of brine or liquid smoke used, and the dehydrator itself, you will need anywhere from 4 to 24 hours to complete the drying process.

The importance of proper drying techniques and temperatures cannot be overstated. Proper drying reduces the external and internal moisture content of the meat to levels that inhibit bacterial activity and growth.

Calibrating Thermometers

Before you move on to the four methods for making jerky, calibrate your thermometers. This may seem tedious, but it is important: make certain the calibration of your dial-stem thermometer is correct. Simply put, you are checking the accuracy of the thermometer that will check your dehydrator. Without an accurate thermometer, any readings you take will lead to wrong assessments of temperature. You should calibrate thermometers before each use and whenever they are dropped. They are sensitive and can lose accuracy from extensive use or when going from one temperature extreme to another. Remember that you are using them with meat, and incorrect cooking temperatures can lead to undercooked jerky that can pose a health risk.

Thermometers can be calibrated by the use of ice water. Use these steps:

- Fill a 2-cup measuring cup with crushed ice and water and stir well.

- Let sit 4 to 5 minutes.

- Completely submerge the sensing area of the thermometer's stem or probe in the ice water, but keep it from touching the sides or bottom of the container.

- Hold for 30 seconds or until the displayed temperature stabilizes.

To calibrate a thermometer, first fill a 2-quart measuring cup with crushed ice. Add water and stir well. Then let sit for 4 minutes to reach a temperature of 32 degrees Fahrenheit.

Place the stem of the thermometer into the water without touching the sides or bottom. Then hold for 30 seconds or until the dial stops moving. Adjust the thermometer if it is not within plus or minus 2 degrees of 32 degrees Fahrenheit. Repeat this process with each thermometer to be used.

- If the thermometer is not within plus or minus 2 degrees of 32 degrees Fahrenheit, adjust the thermometer accordingly. The ice-water method permits calibration within 0.1 degree Fahrenheit. (Some digital stemmed thermometers have a reset button, which makes calibration especially easy.)

- Repeat the process with each thermometer.

- Any food thermometer that cannot be calibrated can still be used by checking it for accuracy using either method described. You can take into consideration any inaccuracies and make adjustments by adding or subtracting the differences, or consider replacing the thermometer.

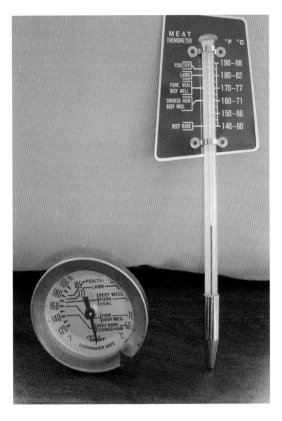

Instant-read thermometers have stems that can be inserted into meat. Those with small probes are easier to use for monitoring meat used for jerky.

Calibrating Your Equipment

Having assured yourself that your thermometer will give you an accurate reading, you are now ready to determine your dehydrator or smoker's drying temperature. Do not test the temperature when the device has meat in it. You will get an inaccurate temperature reading if you do so because of the evaporative cooling that occurs as the meat loses moisture.

For ovens and side-fan dehydrators, you can place a dial-stem thermometer inside the unit and close the door. If your unit is a stacking dehydrator, insert the thermometer between two trays so that the dial sticks out between them.

Next, turn the dehydrator on and to its maximum setting. Once the unit has run for a minimum of 10 minutes, the temperature should stabilize and you can record it. Recheck after another 10 minutes to be certain it has maintained an internal temperature of at least 145 to 155 degrees Fahrenheit. If it does not maintain this temperature, you will need to review the manufacturer's warranty or determine the cause of your unit's failure.

Be aware that most dehydrators equipped with temperature controls and thermostats will cycle around an average temperature at any given setting. For example, at a setting of 155 degrees Fahrenheit, a dehydrator may cool to 150 degrees Fahrenheit and then heat up to 160 degrees Fahrenheit, repeating this cycle every few minutes. That's not necessarily a fault. The popular Excalibur side-fan dehydrators are deliberately designed to do this, as the manufacturer believes that cycling around an average temperature creates a better finished product. Dehydrators that operate with a single, factory-set temperature will tend to maintain a more stable temperature if they are operating correctly.

The University of Wisconsin–Extension actually recommends that you do not use dehydrators with preset factory temperature settings that can't be controlled, as they do not reliably produce a safe product. You can, however, check your dehydrator's ability to reach and hold target temperatures by using a reliable and accurate dial-stem thermometer, placing it inside the dehydrator and checking it several times over 10 minutes to ensure that it can be trusted.

MAKING JERKY WITH A DEHYDRATOR

Although it's possible to make jerky in a conventional oven, I don't recommend it because drying times are long and temperature control is difficult, as you have to keep the oven door partly open to promote air circulation. A convection oven, however, promotes air circulation with a fan and can be used much like a dehydrator to make good jerky. It's best not to dry too much meat at once, however, as most convection ovens do not dry foods as efficiently as dehydrators do. If you use a convection oven to make jerky, use the instructions for making jerky with a high-temperature dehydrator (Method 1).

Method 1: High-Temperature Dehydrator

You Will Need:

- Food dehydrator that can reach temperatures of 160°F or higher

- 2 pounds of meat and a recipe from Chapters 2, 4, 5, or 6

- Equipment used for slicing meat strips

- Drying racks or trays

Instructions

1. Thoroughly wash your hands, countertops, knives, slicers, and any other pieces of equipment you will use.

2. Slice the meat into strips at about ¼ inch thick and prepare per your recipe. Most recipes will require marinating for at least 2 hours or overnight before proceeding.

3. Set out the drying racks or trays, remove the meat strips from the marinade, and place the meat strips close together but not so close that they touch or overlap each other. Place the trays or racks in the dehydrator.

4. Preheat a reliable high-temperature dehydrator to 160°F or slightly higher. Then put in the meat for 4 to 6 hours or until it reaches an internal temperature of 160°F (poultry needs to reach 165°F internal temperature). If you maintain the high temperature, you should not need to lower it to finish the drying process. However, monitor the meat strips' progress so that they do not become too dry.

5. You should begin checking the jerky after 3 hours from the start of the drying process. To test the jerky for doneness, first pat off any beads of oil or fat with a paper towel. The jerky can be considered finished if it cracks when bent over on itself but doesn't break clean through. There is a fine line between underdone and overdone jerky. If it breaks, it has been dried too much. This isn't a disaster—it's still edible. With any new equipment that you use, some experimentation may be necessary to reach a result that is satisfactory to your tastes.

6. After allowing the jerky to cool to room temperature, store it in a clean plastic container with a tight-fitting lid or in a resealable plastic bag, and place the container in the refrigerator. If you notice any condensation forming on the inside of either, the jerky should be returned to the dehydrator and dried a little longer.

Method 2: Oven and Low-Temperature Dehydrator

You Will Need:

- Oven

- Food dehydrator

- 2 pounds of meat and a recipe from Chapter 2, 4, 5, or 6

- Equipment used for slicing meat strips

- Drying racks or trays

Instructions

1. Thoroughly wash your hands, countertops, knives, slicers, and any other pieces of equipment you will use.

2. Slice the meat into strips at about ¼ inch thick and prepare per your recipe. Most recipes will require marinating for at least 2 hours or overnight before proceeding.

3. Preheat your oven to 145 to 155°F. Set out the drying racks or trays, remove the meat strips from the marinade, and place the meat strips close together but not so close that they touch or overlap each other.

4. Once the oven is preheated, place the trays or racks in the oven. Bake the meat for approximately 4 hours. Increase the heat to 275°F and continue to bake until the meat reaches an internal temperature of 160°F (poultry needs to reach 165°F internal temperature).

Jerky that is properly dried should bend a little without breaking but not be so soft that it bends completely.

5. Once the meat reaches an internal temperature of 160°F, you can use a low-temperature dehydrator to finish the drying. Transfer your meat to a dehydrator and maintain a constant dehydrator temperature of 130 to 140°F while you continue drying.

6. You should begin checking the jerky after 3 hours from the start of the drying process to make sure that is doesn't dry past the point where it's enjoyable to eat. To test the jerky for doneness, first pat off any beads of oil or fat with a paper towel. The jerky can be considered finished drying if it cracks—but doesn't break—when it's bent over on itself. There is a fine line between underdone and overdone jerky. If it breaks, it has been overheated. This is not a disaster—it will still be edible—but more of an inconvenience. With any new equipment that you use, some experimentation may be necessary to reach a result that is satisfactory to your tastes.

7. After allowing the jerky to cool to room temperature, store it in a clean plastic container with a tight-fitting lid or in a resealable plastic bag, and place the container in the refrigerator. If you notice any condensation forming on the inside of either, the jerky should be returned to the dehydrator or oven and dried a little longer.

MAKING JERKY WITH A SMOKER

Smoking jerky meat can be done for one of two reasons: it can add smoky flavor and an attractive color to your jerky and/or it can dehydrate your jerky completely—similar to using a high-temperature food dehydrator.

Liquid Smoke

If you're after a smoky flavor, you can, of course, bypass the smoker and use liquid smoke. It can be added to a marinade or dry rub and will adhere

Storing Jerky

Dried jerky can be safely stored for one to two months at room temperature and in the freezer for up to six months.

Do not consume any jerky stored in a container that shows any signs of mold. Dispose of it immediately and rinse any affected container with scalding water first. Then use a sanitizer to thoroughly clean the container and rinse again with scalding water. Be careful when handling any affected pieces by using rubber or plastic gloves and thoroughly wash the gloves after handling moldy pieces or containers. Make certain the affected pieces or containers do not come into contact with counter surfaces or other foods to be consumed. Be sure that when you dispose of any moldy jerky pieces that children or pets are not able to come into contact with them.

Store your dried jerky in glass jars at cool or room temperatures and away from sunlight and humidity, or in the refrigerator.

to the surface of the meat before it's dried. This coating will provide a smoky flavor. It should be used in moderation and in keeping with recipe recommendations to avoid off flavors.

Liquid smoke is commercially produced from smoke created from burning hardwood chips or sawdust such as hickory, apple, or mesquite. It is burned at high temperatures and, as the smoke passes through a condenser, it will cool and when aided by water, will form a liquid. This liquid is then concentrated for a stronger flavor. Liquid smoke is commercially available, and many food outlets sell it as a flavoring and food preservative. It is widely used in foods in which a smoky flavor is desired, such as bacon, smoked cheeses, tofu, and yes, jerky.

Be aware that liquid smoke may contain some residual carcinogens because it is made from real smoke, although commercial producers attempt to remove all smoke condensates, such as tar and ash, during the processing. Some concern has been expressed relating to the different concentrations of polycyclic aromatic hydrocarbons (PAHs) that are found in different liquid smoke flavorings. These concentrations appear to relate to the different types of trees used for the wood or sawdust burned to make the smoke, but they have been found to be within acceptable health levels. Manufacturers filter liquid smoke in their production process, and it's generally considered safe to use, if used in moderation.

Some brands of liquid smoke add seasonings or flavorings, such as vinegar or molasses, as well as caramel and other colorings. Buy a plain liquid smoke product if you do not want these additional flavorings and colorings. You can add your own flavors to the marinade later. Remember to always use liquid smoke in moderation.

Smokers

If you just want to add a smoky flavor to your meat before using a dehydrator, you can use just about any model—even a home grill with a smoke box or smoking attachment will work just fine if the proper temperatures can be reached and maintained for extended periods. Traditional smokers burn wood both to create smoke and to cook the meat. With electric smokers, you will need to add wood chips or pellets to a heating chamber to produce smoke.

Smokers specifically designed for smoking meats, however, do two things at once: they provide a proper temperature to kill harmful pathogens, and they produce a pleasing smoky flavor. The heat used can originate from various sources, including electricity, wood chips or

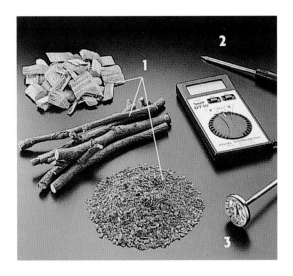

To produce the smoke needed, various woods (1) such as hickory, cherry, apple, and mesquite are used in home smokers. The smoke can be made from chips, tree trimmings, or sawdust. A digital thermometer (2) monitors the internal temperature without having to open the smoker, causing heat loss. An instant-read thermometer (3) monitors the temperature through a vent hole or a hole specifically designed for a thermometer.

pellets, gas, or charcoal briquettes. If you're using wood, different varieties can be used to infuse a unique smoke flavor or finished jerky color (see page 71).

Using a smoker to make jerky will require some trial and error with your particular model. It's safe to say, however, that if you're already quite comfortable with it—if you know how to get it to hit key temperatures and keep it there—you'll be ahead of the game.

No matter your level of familiarity with your smoker, it will require attention and patience to control several variables when making jerky. For example, to provide a good ventilation of the smoke while still maintaining the proper heat, you need to make sure the smoker has proper airflow. Also, while it might seem like a contradiction, it may be necessary to maintain a degree of humidity inside the smoker through the dehydrating process to prevent the meat from getting too dry or too smoky.

Some precautions may be necessary. Typical recommendations suggest smoking the jerky at 200 degrees Fahrenheit for 1.5 to 2 hours with the smoke on, but a little longer if the smoker does not reach that temperature. Don't smoke the meat for more than 3 hours because too much smoke can produce a bitter taste.

The most commonly available home smokers that work for making jerky include vertical electric water smokers, insulated variable-temperature smokers, electric smokers, and stove-top smokers. Your choice of which one to use may be influenced by the amount of indoor space you have available for a smoker, whether you have access to outdoor areas to use them, your budget, and your commitment to long-term use as an investment in a smoker. Understanding their advantages and limitations may help you

decide which is best for your situation. The following are just brief descriptions of a few models, but I encourage you to research all the models that are commercially available to determine which one will work best for you. Their prices range from modest to expensive, and this may give some indication of their durability. Some are stationary, while others may be set on rollers for easier movement. They may be rectangular or round, and the number of trays increases with larger units. Many different types of digitally controlled smoker models are available and popular because they allow you to easily monitor the temperature and time.

Depending on the model used, one concern about smokers is the potential loss of heat caused by opening a door to add water to a pan or to replenish wood chips or pellets. Models are available that have external wood chip or pellet loaders so the unit doesn't need to be opened. A smoker like the Masterbuilt Electric Smoker has a tray that can be pulled out, have fresh chips or pellets added to it, and be pushed back into the unit without opening the door. (This is an outdoor model not meant for inside use.)

Vertical electric water smokers are popular because they are generally the least expensive smokers on the market, although the cheaper models are not recommended for making jerky because they cannot reach the high temperatures required. They work well for vegetables and other non-meat foods. The more expensive models, like the Weber Smokey Mountain, have better temperature control. These units have either a gas or electric heat source and typically have three components. The bottom is the heat source. Above this is a water pan that stores heat and regulates the internal temperature. Above the water pan is the smoking chamber. The biggest disadvantage is the loss of heat when the lid is opened. To prevent this, you will need a thermometer that can signal the temperature to an outside receiver.

An insulated variable-temperature smoker has good temperature control. This variety is becoming more popular with people who want to do home-smoking. They are typically more expensive than other models but are easy to use and generally conform to the same dynamics as a vertical electric water smoker.

Electric smokers are another popular type because they are easy to use and don't take up a lot of space. The more expensive models typically have a rheostat that turns down the electricity flow to the coil, much like that found on an electric stove or hot plate, and they may have multiple settings ranging from low to high. Some of the more expensive electric smokers have thermostats that have a temperature probe inside the cooking chamber. The thermostat monitors the temperature and will raise it if it's too low or lower it if it's too high. This makes a unit with a thermostat better than one with a rheostat but also makes the unit more expensive. Remember, however, that unless you can control the temperature, you can't produce safe jerky. This variety's main drawback is that they don't work well outdoors in cold weather.

Stovetop smokers, such as the Cameron stovetop models, have become available in recent years and may solve your budget, space, and storage concerns. The stainless steel unit is an enclosed system that uses your stovetop for heat to activate the flavored wood chips that are sprinkled across the inside bottom of the pan. The meat is placed on a grill rack that is set above the base. The cover tightly seals in the heat and smoke. Stovetop smokers work well in apartments or places where other smoking units can't be used. They are inexpensive, easy to use and clean, and will work well with beef, fish, poultry, wild game, and waterfowl. One drawback of these units is their small size, as most range between 7 and 11 inches wide and 11 and 15 inches long, limiting the amount of meat they can hold at one time.

Powering Your Smoker

A vertical water smoker is built with a bottom fire pan that holds wood chips or small briquettes and generally has two cooking racks near the top. The water pan positioned above the coals supplies moisture and helps regulate the internal temperature. An electric smoker is similar, except the smoke is produced by premoistened wood chips rather than by charcoal. The electrical element provides a more constant temperature and may require less attention during smoking. The size of electric smokers varies, with some accommodating several pounds of meat at one time.

Electric smokers are less likely to overheat and thus simply cook the meat because they can be more precisely controlled than any other type of smoker. If you're purchasing an electric smoker and want to use it for jerky, make sure it has adjustable temperature controls that can reach 160 degrees Fahrenheit (165 degrees Fahrenheit if you intend to smoke poultry) or higher.

While wood or charcoal can be used for powering more traditional smokers, charcoal briquettes are difficult to use for jerky-making because they need to be kept at a constant and consistent burning rate for the 10 hours required.

Electric smokers are popular because they are easy to use and reliable. There are stovetop smokers that can also be used.

Selecting the type of wood to use for smoking jerky meat is more a matter of personal preference than anything. Your choice will affect the flavor and often the color of the finished product. In a smoker, the smoke rises from the combustion area into the cooking area. Essentially, the smoke particles attach to the outer surface of the meat because the particles move or migrate from a warm surface (chamber) to a cold surface (meat).

Even if you like the flavor of smoke, don't overdo it. Too much smoke can make the meat taste bitter or like ash. Each smoker is different, and you may have to test several batches until you reach a flavor that suits you. Start light and work your way up incrementally. Keep records of your experiments in a cooking log.

The best woods for smoking are cured (dried) hardwoods with a low sap flow, such as fruit and nut woods. These can be divided into two basic groups that are based not on wood species, but whether they yield a mild or strong flavor.

- For mild smoke flavors, use alder, apple, cherry, maple, orange, or peach woods.

- Strong flavors come from hickory, oak, mesquite, pecan, and walnut.

Avoid using conifer woods, such as pine, cedar, spruce, and fir. They contain too much sap, and because of their high tar content, they can produce a bitter flavor. Also, use only air-dried woods and *never* use moldy wood, which may contain toxins. Many of the woods you use for smoking can be purchased at specialty stores, outdoor outlets, or dried by yourself.

The wood used to create the smoke usually needs to be soaked in water before it goes into the smoker. That will prevent it from burning. Burning wood will create some smoke, of course, but not enough for your purpose. If you're using a small smoking unit, you will likely be using very small wood chips or sawdust rather than chunks of wood. These can just be sprayed with water from a mister bottle. If using larger wood chips or chunks, however, soak them in water for at least an hour before using them. The idea is to create smoke rather than flame, and to add flavor rather than heat.

Depending on where you place your smoking unit, make sure there is adequate ventilation so that any escaping heat and smoke does not create air-quality problems, such as carbon monoxide in your home, shed, or apartment. Carbon monoxide is an invisible, odorless gas that can be produced by malfunctioning appliances, such as gas- or wood-burning stoves, fireplaces, and smokers. Carbon monoxide alarms are available, and you should have one installed inside your home if you use a smoker.

Method 3:
Smoker and Low-Temperature Dehydrator

You Will Need:

- Smoker (outdoor model)

- Food dehydrator

- 2 pounds of meat and a recipe from Chapter 2, 4, 5, or 6

- Equipment used for slicing meat strips

- Drying racks or trays

Instructions

1. Thoroughly wash your hands, countertops, knives, slicers, and any other pieces of equipment you will use.

2. Slice the meat into strips at about ¼ inch thick and prepare per your recipe. Some recipes may require marinating for at least 2 hours or overnight before proceeding.

3. Preheat your smoker to 200°F. Add chips or pellets to the burn chamber to begin smoking. Use the smoker vents to stabilize the temperature between 165 and 175°F.

4. Set out the drying racks or trays. Remove the meat strips from the refrigerator and the marinade. Pat the strips dry and place them close together—but not so close that they touch or overlap each other.

5. Place the rack or racks with your meat in the smoker. Insert a temperature probe into the thickest piece of meat.

6. Smoke the meat for 4 to 6 hours or to an internal temperature of 160°F (or 165°F for poultry). The amount of time smoke is added to the heating chamber will depend on personal preference, but 3 hours should be sufficient. If you prefer a heavy smoke, you can allow more time. You may have to experiment with the smoking process to determine the amount that suits your tastes. Add water to the pan if needed—although you are dehydrating the meat, it may be necessary to maintain humidity inside the smoker to prevent it from getting too dry or too smoky.

7. Once the meat reaches an internal temperature of 160°F, you can use a low-temperature dehydrator to finish the drying. Transfer the meat to the dehydrator and maintain a constant dehydrator temperature of 130 to 140°F while you continue drying.

8. Test the jerky for doneness after 4 hours. First pat off any beads of oil or fat with a paper towel. The jerky is finished if you can bend it over on itself and it cracks but doesn't break. There is a fine line between underdone and overdone jerky. If it breaks, it has been dried too much. This is not a disaster—it will still be edible—but more of an inconvenience. With any new equipment that you use, some experimentation may be necessary to reach a result that is satisfactory to your tastes.

9. After allowing the jerky to cool to room temperature, store it in a clean plastic container with a tight-fitting lid or in a resealable plastic

bag, and place the container in the refrigerator. If you notice any condensation forming on the inside of either, the jerky should be returned to the dehydrator and dried a little longer.

Method 4: Smoker

You Will Need:

- Smoker (electrically powered)

- 2 pounds of meat and a recipe from Chapter 2, 4, 5, or 6

- Equipment used for slicing meat strips

- Drying racks or trays

Instructions

1. Thoroughly wash your hands, countertops, knives, slicers, and any other pieces of equipment you will use.

2. Slice the meat into strips at about ¼ inch thick and prepare per your recipe. Most recipes used in this book require marinating for at least 2 hours or overnight before proceeding.

3. Preheat your empty smoker to 200°F and hold at 175 to 180°F for 15 to 20 minutes. Add water to the pan as well as seasonings (if desired).

4. Set out the drying racks or trays. Remove the meat strips from the refrigerator and the marinade. Pat the strips dry and place them on the racks so that they're close together, but not so close that they touch or overlap each other.

5. Place the rack or racks with your meat in the smoker. Insert a temperature probe into the thickest piece of meat.

6. Heat the meat for 4 to 6 hours or to an internal meat temperature of 160°F. You may wish to rotate the racks after 2 hours to ensure even heating.

7. After the internal temperature reaches 160°F (165°F for poultry), begin adding smoke to the heating chamber with wood pellets or chips in the chamber designed to hold them. The amount of time smoke is added to the heating chamber will depend on personal preference, but 3 hours should be sufficient. If you prefer a heavy smoke, you can allow more time. You may have to experiment with the smoking process to determine the amount that suits your tastes.

8. Test the jerky for doneness after 4 hours. First pat off any beads of oil or fat with a paper towel. The jerky is considered finished if you can bend it over on itself and it cracks but doesn't break. There is a fine line between underdone and overdone jerky. If it breaks, it has been overheated. This is not a casualty—it will still be edible—but more of an inconvenience. With any new equipment that you use, some experimentation may be necessary to reach a result that is satisfactory to your tastes.

9. Remove the racks from the smoker. After allowing the jerky to cool to room temperature, store it in a clean plastic container with a tight-fitting lid or in a resealable plastic bag, and place the container in the refrigerator. If you notice any condensation forming on the inside of either, the jerky should be returned to the smoker and dried a little longer.

Chapter 4

BEEF AND VENISON JERKY

While almost any animal can be a source for jerky meat, beef is still the most popular choice. Since processing venison is similar to beef, and since venison jerky is also a popular choice, we'll consider both in this chapter. In fact, cows, deer, elk, and even moose have similar substantial muscle components that can be cut into strips for jerky, especially when compared to smaller animals and fowl such as rabbits, wild turkey, ducks, and geese.

For processing, the similarities don't end there. These animals all have four legs, a comparable skeletal structure, and similar muscle structures. Because their muscle locations are similar, they lend themselves to similar cutting and carcass deconstruction processes. The main difference is in the amount of muscle that is found on either carcass.

The quantity of the muscles available from similar areas may be different depending on the animal, and there may be texture differences in the muscles due to their diets. Domestically raised beef often have access to more feed that is more nutritious than that available to wild animals. While genetics may also have some effect, none of these, however, need alter your method for processing the meat into jerky.

SELECTING AND PREPARING BEEF

Beef is the favorite meat for making jerky, especially in North America, and it is readily available to most people. While many beef cuts are offered for sale in markets and grocery stores, it is the leanest portions—those with the least amount of fat in them—that are the best for making jerky. An increase in the fat level makes the jerky harder to dry, and it also can cause a reduction in the time it can be successfully stored.

Fat is useful in meat cuts that are cooked traditionally because it increases the flavor. It can add to the flavor of the jerky, too, but cuts that contain a large portion of fat streaks—called marbling—should be avoided if a leaner cut is available. Typically, the best or most expensive cuts of beef originate along the backbone, such as the tenderloin, because as its name indicates, it is more tender than other cuts. This is a result of less muscle movement than other cuts such as the round, which is found in the rear quarters of the animal, or the brisket, which is found in the front.

Range-fed animals, whether they are beef, bison, sheep, goats, or other domestic species, tend to have less of an overall fat content in their muscles due to a leaner diet with decreased levels of grains such as corn and more frequent movement than those fed for market purposes in feedlots.

Bison are similar to domestic beef in their muscle and skeletal structure and body size. Native wild herds of bison are likely not going to be your meat source, though. But bison meat can be sourced from farms that raise them in more controlled conditions, although still not in confined feedlots. Because of their ranging and herding instincts, bison must be allowed movement to areas open to roaming. Bison yield a very lean, red meat that can be turned into excellent jerky.

Beef and bison have similar meat cuts, although bison almost always contains less fat. This is largely due to genetics and partly to diet. Both have huge fore- and hindquarters, loins, bellies, briskets and other similar parts of their bodies from which cuts can be drawn. An illustration of where the cuts are sourced can be useful in determining which you may want to use (see right).

Quartering

Any quadruped animal carcass can be divided into quarters: the two forequarters and two hindquarters. Each forequarter consists of five major cuts: chuck, rib, brisket, plate, and shank. The hindquarter contains the most valuable retail cuts, including the round, loin, and flank.

After slaughter, skinning, and dressing, a beef or bison carcass is split in half to divide it into more manageable quantities. Each is called a "half" or "side" of beef or bison. The live weight of the animal will determine the size of the dressed carcass. After the internal organs, hide, and head are removed in the butchering process, the amount that is left is called the carcass weight.

This weight is often expressed as a percentage of the live weight. The dressing percentage is the proportion of the live weight that remains in the carcass and is sometimes referred to as "yield." It is calculated as follows: the carcass weight divided by the live weight times 100 equals dressing percentage. For example, if a beef animal's live weight is 1,200 pounds and the resulting carcass weight (both halves) equals 780 pounds, it would have a dressing percentage of 65 percent, which is within a standard range.

Why is this important? The reason to understand these numbers or the calculation method is to acquaint you with the poundage of meat involved if working with a live animal you raise or may consider buying from a producer if you choose to cut up your own carcass.

In our example, one-half side of a beef/bison would weigh 390 pounds (780 ÷ 2). A "quarter" of

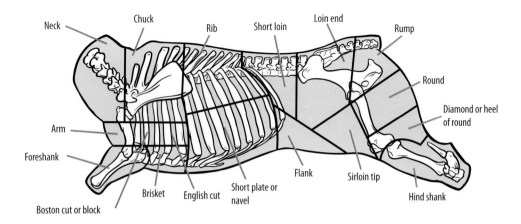

Neck · Chuck · Rib · Short loin · Loin end · Rump · Round · Diamond or heel of round · Arm · Foreshank · Boston cut or block · Brisket · English cut · Short plate or navel · Flank · Sirloin tip · Hind shank

A beef anatomy can be broken down into imaginary cuts while still alive. Studying the drawing and comparing it to a live animal will lead to better understanding of the structure when the slaughter process begins.

this animal alone would weigh 195 pounds. Unless you purchased an already processed animal, you will have a large quantity of meat to handle.

Of course, not all of the carcass would be made into jerky. Different parts of the carcass create different cuts, including steaks, loin eyes, and ground beef. A basic description of the typical cuts available from each section of the carcass will help you understand the best places from which to derive your jerky meat.

Forequarters: The forequarters are considered the portion of the carcass from the twelfth rib forward to the neck. This will include the brisket, chuck, and foreshanks, which are the upper portions of the front legs.

The brisket is that portion above and between the front legs. The chuck is the largest cut on a beef animal, and the two right and left pieces will account for about 25 percent of the total carcass weight. The chuck contains a lot of connective tissue because of the exercise it receives to provide movement for the animal. The chuck is often made into roasts. There is a considerable amount of lean trim, however, that can be used for jerky.

The foreshank and brisket are considered rough cuts but make up about one-quarter

of the total carcass weight. The plate of the forequarter is the lowest part of the ribs but does not include part of the brisket. This will contain the diaphragm muscle that controls the animal's breathing. This is an excellent piece for jerky, although if purchased at a supermarket, it may not always be available because of its demand in restaurants as a skirt steak.

Hindquarters: The hindquarters portion of the carcass is located from the twelfth rib back to the tail. It includes the round, loin, and flank, and will compose about half of the carcass weight. There is a considerable amount of meat found in the hindquarters and most all of it will make excellent jerky. Portions can be cut along the natural divisions or seams created between the muscles and connective tissue and then sliced into strips. When large quantities of jerky are planned, it may be best to purchase a hindquarter or whole leg and cut it yourself.

Although the loin is considered part of the hindquarters, it runs along the backbone. This muscle area requires minimal movement which in turn makes it very tender and very desirable for steaks. This makes it too expensive a cut to turn into jerky from domestic animals. Also, it typically has a higher fat content that does not make it as adaptable for jerky. Use the loin cuts for steaks rather than jerky.

The round contains a sizable portion of the hindquarters and is often broken down into different retail cuts including the top round, bottom round, top sirloin, rump, sirloin tip, hind shank, and heel of round.

The entire round can be separated from the rest of the hindquarter by cutting through the femur, a large bone in the thigh, at the rear of the pelvic bone. Once the round is separated from the loin, it is fairly easy to cut up for jerky. The name of each cut is derived from its position when the round is laid on a table.

The top round is also called the inside round because in its natural position it would be on the interior side of the live animal. This cut is lean and has a fine muscle grain that makes it very desirable for jerky.

The bottom round is also called the outside round because that is its position when it is placed on a table for cutting—it is on the bottom. This portion contains more fibrous tissue than the top round but can be cut into strips for jerky. The top and bottom round include several muscle groups with different striations and can be cut either with or against the grain for jerky.

The sirloin tip is a large cut that lies in front of the femur, or thigh bone, in the standing animal and is composed of four muscles. The top round and sirloin tip are more tender than the bottom round and the eye and will make good jerky.

The heel of round, or sometimes called the eye of round, is a boneless cut and the smallest muscle in the hind leg. It is a triangular piece located between the bottom round and the top round and is separated from the other muscles by natural seams. It is likely to be the least tender cut. For use in jerky, it is usually cut with the grain into strips, or

A side of beef refers to one-half of the animal's carcass. The rear quarters, located at the top of this hanging side of beef, are typically made into roasts or ground round. Because the rear quarter is lean, it is also a good source of jerky meat.

across the grain into small steaks. These can then be cut into strips or cubes for jerky making.

The rump is considered as part of the round and can make up about four percent of the carcass weight. Because it is often cut into roasts, you can use it for slicing jerky strips as well.

Flank: The flank is composed of the abdominal muscles of the animal and runs under the belly and from side to side below and posterior to the ribs. The flank muscles hold all the internal organs in the correct position. Flank steaks can be cut from each side of the carcass and can be further cut into strips for jerky either with the grain of the muscle or across the grain.

The general rule is the larger the animal, regardless of species, the more meat you will have for processing. As the size of the skeletal structure increases, so do the muscles to accommodate movement regardless of how much fat is interlaced through them. All muscle has some fat because it's an energy source. The amount of that fat is dependent on diet and the extent of the animal's movement.

BAR-B-QUE JERKY

4 POUNDS LEAN BEEF, SLICED INTO ¼-INCH-THICK STRIPS

MARINADE

1 cup ketchup or tomato sauce

½ cup red wine vinegar

¼ cup light brown sugar

2 tablespoons Worcestershire sauce

2 tablespoons salt

1 tablespoon dry mustard

½ tablespoon onion powder

1 teaspoon ground black pepper

⅛ teaspoon Tabasco sauce

In a nonmetallic container, thoroughly mix the tomato sauce, vinegar, brown sugar, Worcestershire sauce, salt, mustard, onion powder, black pepper, and Tabasco sauce. Add the meat and coat all sides. Cover the container and refrigerate for at least 10 hours. Using one of the four methods in Chapter 3 (starting on page 58), dry the meat. Make sure the meat reaches an internal temperature of 160°F. Remove, let cool, and store in sealed jars in the refrigerator.

HONEYED JERKY

2 POUNDS LEAN BEEF, SLICED INTO ¼-INCH-THICK STRIPS

MARINADE

½ cup soy sauce

½ cup honey

¼ cup fresh lemon juice

2 cloves garlic, minced

1 teaspoon ground black pepper

In a nonmetallic container, thoroughly mix the soy sauce, honey, lemon juice, minced garlic, and black pepper. Dip the meat strips into the marinade mixture and put them in a nonmetallic container. Pour the marinade over strips, cover the container, and refrigerate for 2 to 4 hours. Rotate the strips half way through the marinade time. Using one of the four methods in Chapter 3 (starting on page 58), dry the meat. Make sure the meat reaches an internal temperature of 160°F. Remove, let cool, and store in sealed jars in the refrigerator.

DRY QUICK JERKY

2 POUNDS LEAN BEEF, SLICED INTO ¼-INCH-THICK STRIPS

DRY MIX

1 tablespoon Morton Tender Quick

2 teaspoons sugar

1 teaspoon ground black pepper

1 teaspoon garlic powder

In a nonmetallic container, thoroughly mix the Morton Tender Quick, sugar, black pepper, and garlic powder. Rub the slices of meat on all sides with the dry mix. Place coated meat strips in a plastic bag and seal. Refrigerate for 1 hour. Using one of the four methods in Chapter 3 (starting on page 58), dry the meat. Make sure the meat reaches an internal temperature of 160°F. Remove, let cool, and store in sealed jars in the refrigerator.

LOW-SALT PEPPER JERKY

2 POUNDS LEAN BEEF, SLICED INTO ¼-INCH-THICK STRIPS

MARINADE

1 cup low-salt soy sauce

¼ cup liquid smoke

2 tablespoons ground black pepper

In a nonmetallic container, thoroughly mix the soy sauce and liquid smoke. Place the meat strips in marinade, cover the container, and refrigerate for 4 hours. Place the meat strips on dehydrator or oven rack. Using a shaker, sprinkle the pepper on one side of the meat, then turn strips over and sprinkle on other side. Using one of the four methods in Chapter 3 (starting on page 58), dry the meat. Make sure the meat reaches an internal temperature of 160°F. Remove, let cool, and store in sealed jars in the refrigerator.

TERIYAKI JERKY

2 POUNDS LEAN BEEF, SLICED INTO ¼-INCH-THICK STRIPS

MARINADE

½ cup soy sauce

¼ cup light brown sugar

2 cloves garlic, minced

1 tablespoon salt

1 tablespoon ground ginger

½ teaspoon ground black pepper

½ teaspoon liquid smoke (optional)

In a nonmetallic container, thoroughly mix the soy sauce, brown sugar, minced garlic, salt, ginger, pepper, and liquid smoke, if desired, and allow at least 15 minutes for flavors to blend. Add the strips individually, and turn and coat both sides with sauce. Cover and marinate in the refrigerator for 8 to 10 hours. Using one of the four methods in Chapter 3 (starting on page 58), dry the meat. Make sure the meat reaches an internal temperature of 160°F. Remove, let cool, and store in sealed jars in the refrigerator.

SESAME SEED JERKY

2 POUNDS LEAN BEEF, SLICED INTO ¼-INCH-THICK STRIPS

MARINADE

½ cup soy sauce

½ cup sherry or dry vermouth

¼ cup sesame seeds

1 tablespoon light brown sugar

1 tablespoon salt

½ teaspoon ground black pepper

In a nonmetallic container, thoroughly mix soy sauce, sherry, sesame seeds, brown sugar, salt, and black pepper until the sugar and salt have dissolved. Place the strips in mixture to cover both sides. Cover and marinate in the refrigerator overnight. You can turn the strips before bedtime and after rising in the morning before removing. Using one of the four methods in Chapter 3 (starting on page 58), dry the meat. Make sure the meat reaches an internal temperature of 160°F. Remove, let cool, and store in sealed jars in the refrigerator.

HAWAIIAN ISLAND JERKY

2 POUNDS LEAN BEEF, SLICED INTO ¼-INCH-THICK STRIPS

MARINADE

½ cup pineapple juice

½ cup soy sauce

2 cloves garlic, crushed

2 tablespoons light brown sugar

1 tablespoon ginger

1 tablespoon salt

1 teaspoon ground black pepper

½ teaspoon cayenne pepper

In a nonmetallic container, thoroughly mix the pineapple juice, soy sauce, crushed garlic, sugar, ginger, salt, black pepper, and cayenne pepper until sugar is completely dissolved. Dip the meat strips into the marinade, covering both sides. Cover and refrigerate 6 to 8 hours. Using one of the four methods in Chapter 3 (starting on page 58), dry the meat. Make sure the meat reaches an internal temperature of 160°F. Remove, let cool, and store in sealed jars in the refrigerator.

CHINA JERKY

2 POUNDS LEAN BEEF, SLICED INTO ¼-INCH-THICK STRIPS

MARINADE

1 cup sugar

½ cup soy sauce

¼ cup ketchup

¼ cup hoisin sauce

¼ cup oyster sauce

¼ cup honey

¼ cup sake, sherry, or dry vermouth

2 tablespoons salt

In a nonmetallic container, thoroughly mix sugar, soy sauce, ketchup, hoisin sauce, oyster sauce, honey, sake, and salt until sugar and honey are completely dissolved. Place meat strips in the marinade, submerging completely, then cover and refrigerate for 24 hours. Using one of the four methods in Chapter 3 (starting on page 58), dry the meat. Make sure the meat reaches an internal temperature of 160°F. Remove, let cool, and store in sealed jars in the refrigerator.

DRIED-HERB JERKY

2 POUNDS LEAN BEEF, SLICED INTO ¼-INCH-THICK STRIPS

DRY RUB

1 tablespoon salt

1 teaspoon onion salt

½ teaspoon garlic salt

½ teaspoon lemon-pepper seasoning salt

½ teaspoon oregano

½ teaspoon basil

½ teaspoon marjoram

½ teaspoon thyme

In a nonmetallic container, thoroughly mix salt, onion salt, garlic salt, lemon-pepper seasoning salt, oregano, basil, marjoram, and thyme. Place the meat strips on clean, hard cutting surface and sprinkle one-half of the dry rub over one side. Pound the strips with a meat mallet or tenderizer to work in the spices. Turn the strips over and sprinkle with the rest of the dry rub. Pound the strips with a meat mallet or tenderizer. Arrange the strips on oven racks or dehydrator trays and dry at 160°F for 4 hours. Then turn the strips over and dry for another 4 to 6 hours, or until the jerky is done. Remove, let cool, and then individually wrap each piece in wax paper and store in a sealed container.

FRIED THAI JERKY

2 POUNDS LEAN BEEF, SLICED INTO ¼-INCH-THICK STRIPS

MARINADE

3 tablespoons whole coriander seeds

1 tablespoon cumin seeds

¼ cup soy sauce

1½ tablespoons light brown sugar

1½ cup peanut oil

Toast the coriander and cumin seeds in a hot skillet for 3 to 4 minutes over medium heat. Cool the seeds and grind them to a powder. In a nonmetallic container, mix the soy sauce, coriander and cumin, and brown sugar until the sugar is completely dissolved. Add the meat strips and coat both sides. Cover the container and marinate for at 1 hour in the refrigerator. Using one of the four methods in Chapter 3 (starting on page 58), dry the meat. Make sure the meat reaches an internal temperature of 160°F. Remove and let cool. Heat peanut oil in a pan on medium heat. Fry the dried jerky strips several at a time until they're crispy around the edges. Remove the strips and place on paper towels to cool. Once cooled, store them in an airtight container or in the refrigerator. Serve as snack or with cooked rice as a meal.

HONEY-MUSTARD JERKY

5 POUNDS LEAN BEEF, SLICED INTO ¼-INCH-THICK STRIPS

MARINADE

2½ cups soy sauce

½ cup honey

2 tablespoons prepared mustard

2 tablespoons onion juice

1 tablespoon salt

In a medium bowl, thoroughly mix soy sauce, honey, mustard, onion juice, and salt. Place the meat strips in a nonmetallic container, pour the marinade over them, and stir until well coated. Cover and marinate for 2 hours in the refrigerator. Using one of the four methods in Chapter 3 (starting on page 58), dry the meat. Make sure the meat reaches an internal temperature of 160°F. Remove, let cool, and store in sealed jars in the refrigerator.

JERKY NUGGETS

5 POUNDS LEAN BEEF, CUT INTO 1-INCH CUBES

DRY RUB

1 cup salt

½ cup brown sugar

1 tablespoon ground black pepper

Place the 1-inch meat cubes in a nonmetallic container. Mix the salt, sugar, and pepper together in a small bowl. Sprinkle the dry rub evenly over the meat and coat all sides. Cover and refrigerate for 48 hours, stirring the meat every 12 hours. After 48 hours, remove the meat from the container and rinse with fresh, cold water. Pat the cubes dry and arrange on oven racks or dehydrator trays. Using one of the four methods in Chapter 3 (starting on page 58), dry the meat. Make sure the meat reaches an internal temperature of 160°F by spot-checking two or three of your thickest cubes. Remove, let cool, and store in sealed jars in the refrigerator.

SMOKY JERKY

5 POUNDS LEAN BEEF, SLICED INTO ¼-INCH-THICK STRIPS

MARINADE

1 cup liquid smoke

1 cup Worcestershire sauce

1 cup soy sauce

2 tablespoons salt

½ tablespoon ground black pepper

1 tablespoon garlic powder

In a nonmetallic container, thoroughly mix the liquid smoke, Worcestershire sauce, soy sauce, salt, pepper, and garlic powder. Add the meat strips and coat evenly on both sides. Cover and marinate in the refrigerator for 8 hours or overnight. Using one of the four methods in Chapter 3 (starting on page 58), dry the meat. Make sure the meat reaches an internal temperature of 160°F. Remove, let cool, and store in sealed jars in the refrigerator.

SWEET PICKLE JERKY

5 POUNDS LEAN BEEF, SLICED INTO ¼-INCH-THICK STRIPS

MARINADE

1 gallon hot water

1 cup salt

½ cup light brown sugar

2 tablespoons ground black pepper

½ tablespoon ground allspice

In a nonmetallic container, mix the water, salt, brown sugar, pepper, and allspice until the salt and sugar are dissolved. Place the meat strips in the container and stir to coat thoroughly. Cover and marinate in the refrigerator for 8 hours or overnight. Drain the strips and rinse with clean water. Using one of the four methods in Chapter 3 (starting on page 58), dry the meat. Make sure the meat reaches an internal temperature of 160°F. Remove, let cool, and store in sealed jars in the refrigerator.

CHILI JERKY

5 POUNDS LEAN BEEF, SLICED INTO ¼-INCH-THICK STRIPS

MARINADE

½ cup chili powder

¼ cup salt

½ tablespoon ground black pepper

½ tablespoon freshly ground cumin seeds

½ tablespoon garlic powder

¼ tablespoon cayenne pepper

In a nonmetallic container, thoroughly mix chili powder, salt, pepper, cumin, garlic powder, and cayenne powder. Place the strips in the dry mix and rub the mix into the meat on all sides. Place in a separate, clean container, cover, and refrigerate for 8 hours or overnight. Using one of the four methods in Chapter 3 (starting on page 58), dry the meat. Make sure the meat reaches an internal temperature of 160°F. Remove, let cool, and store in sealed jars in the refrigerator.

HOT WORCESTER JERKY

5 POUNDS LEAN BEEF, SLICED INTO ¼-INCH-THICK STRIPS

MARINADE

1½ cups soy sauce

1 cup Worcestershire sauce

4 tablespoons liquid smoke

2 tablespoons ground black pepper

In a nonmetallic container, thoroughly mix the soy sauce, Worcestershire sauce, liquid smoke, and black pepper. Place the meat strips in the container and completely cover with marinade. Cover the container and refrigerate for 8 hours or overnight. Using one of the four methods in Chapter 3 (starting on page 58), dry the meat. Make sure the meat reaches an internal temperature of 160°F. Remove, let cool, and store in sealed jars in the refrigerator.

PROCESSING VENISON, MOOSE, AND ELK

Deer, moose, and elk are similar to a cow in the location of muscles that can be used for making jerky. Generally their muscles are smaller and may be leaner, with less fat surrounding them or interlaced within the muscles due to their extensive activity as they move about to forage or for flight.

Generally speaking, the largest muscles in wild cervids will be found in the hindquarters. These muscles are used to propel the animals across variable terrain and will receive the most exercise. This, coupled with a leaner diet than domestic animals often have, will affect the quality and quantity of meat that can be derived from them. Although venison has become a more restricted term used for deer meat, for this discussion it will also include moose, elk, and antelope.

Along with beef and bison, venison in the United States can be kosher because cervids are ruminants and possess completely split hooves. These are two of the requirements for land animals. While the processing would need to adhere to appropriate requirements, the source of the meat allows it to qualify for kosher.

There are some thirty species of deer roaming wild around the world. No matter the species, the best meat for making jerky is derived from the hind legs and loin. The shoulders and other parts can be used for strips, or they can be ground up and formed into strips for jerky. You can cut the loins and tenderloins with the grain of the muscle for strips or thin slices or across the grain for medallions. With venison, the highest volume of meat will come from the hind leg or round.

Field Dressing Deer

Deconstructing a deer carcass is much the same as the steps used for a cow, only they are smaller. However, larger animals such as moose, elk, and antelope will typically weigh much more than deer. Either way, the primary concern with field dressing is safety, and you should always take the following precautions:

- Wear disposable rubber gloves when field dressing.

- If your animal is sampled for CWD testing, wait for the test results before processing or eating the meat.

- Do not handle or consume the meat from any animal that exhibits symptoms of CWD.

- Do not eat or cut into the eyes, brain, spinal cord, spleen, tonsils, or lymph nodes of any deer, elk, or moose, and minimize handling of these parts while working on the carcass.

After downing a deer, moose, elk, antelope, or other big-game animal, your primary concern is to cool the carcass down as quickly as possible to prevent the initiation and growth of spoilage bacteria. It also helps prevent the muscle from retaining heat, which affects meat quality. This cooling is especially important if the outside temperature is moderate or warm rather than cool or cold. The faster a deer carcass can be field dressed, the better the meat will likely be. By opening the abdomen and removing the internal organs, the carcass has more opportunity to cool, as air can circulate throughout the body cavity.

The field dressing of a deer as compared to that of a moose, elk, or antelope is similar in many aspects. The greatest differences are likely related to the distance from a populated area you might hunt these animals: moose or elk are hunted in more remote areas than deer. Distance presents a different set of challenges related to transport of the carcass, temperature considerations, and, perhaps, your ability to physically handle these dynamics.

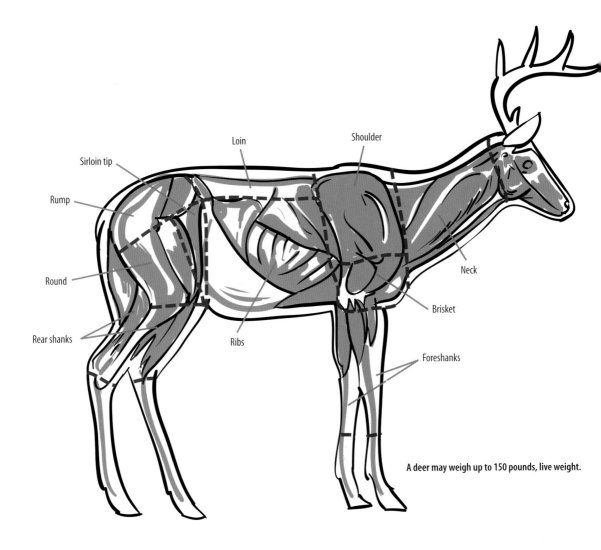

Loin

Shoulder

Sirloin tip

Rump

Round

Rear shanks

Ribs

Neck

Brisket

Foreshanks

A deer may weigh up to 150 pounds, live weight.

It is likely that you will have companions if hunting in a remote area for elk, moose, antelope, or other big-game animals, and this will make handling a large carcass easier. However, if you plan to hunt alone, you should take some precautions prior to entering a remote area. These include providing plans, maps, and timetables to your family or friends; being able to carry in equipment for field dressing; developing and preparing a plan for field dressing any animal you kill; having a plan to safely remove any carcass from the field for processing; and being physically capable of doing these things. You open the possibility of either taking home spoiled meat or not being able to return home alive if you are not able to satisfy these conditions.

There are pros and cons on whether to remove the hide or retain it for a few days depending on whether you are hunting in a remote area or in one closer to home or a populated area. If the animal needs to be dragged from less accessible areas to where it can be properly dressed, retaining the hide will help protect the carcass from dirt or insects. Also, an intact hide prevents surface muscles from drying too quickly. In dusty terrain, you should tie the eviscerated body cavity shut to prevent possible contamination. There are many guides available to help you learn about field dressing a deer, elk, moose, or antelope, including *The Hunter's Guide to Butchering, Smoking & Curing Wild Game and Fish* (see Resources, page 140).

Other Considerations

One significant difference between securing meat from domestically raised beef or bison and those in the wild is that a license, with some exceptions, is required for hunting or fishing. While some specialty grocers may focus on accessing these meats through domestic sources (each of which requires inspection by USDA field inspectors), non-retail game meats are most often obtained through hunting and subsequent slaughter in the field.

Each state has primary responsibility and authority over the hunting of wildlife within its state boundaries. You should learn the rules and regulations that apply in your state. These can be obtained from the state wildlife agencies that sell hunting licenses.

Processing Venison

After field dressing, you will need to cut the carcass up for processing it into smaller portions. There are many ways to do this, and *The Hunter's Guide to Butchering, Smoking & Curing Wild Game & Fish* is a valuable guide that will take you through an extensive step-by-step discussion of how to deconstruct a deer, moose, or elk carcass for your use. However, the brief discussion here

How Much Meat Is There?

The amount of edible meat obtained from a big-game carcass can be estimated before it is dressed. Differences may exist in age or diet of the animal, but the percentages will remain fairly constant. For example, a 100-pound, field-dressed deer will typically dress out at about 80 percent, yielding a carcass that weighs 80 pounds. The typical deer carcass will cut out at 50 percent, meaning half will be meat and the other various parts will be discarded.

This example will then yield forty pounds of edible meat. The rest will be bone, fat, and likely some mutilated areas resulting from shot and blood damage. On the other end of the spectrum, a 1,200-pound moose dressing out at 80 percent will yield a carcass weight of about 960 pounds or roughly 480 pounds of edible meat.

will help you accomplish your task of cutting up a carcass so that you can use it for jerky making.

The loins of these animals are often highly prized for making into steaks rather than jerky. They are located on the underside of the spine and on both sides of the carcass. They are very tender because these muscles receive many of the same nutrients as other muscles do when the animal is feeding but receive very little exercise. They have the most flavor without the toughness of other muscles.

The foreshanks, neck, brisket, and belly are more often trimmed for their meat to be made into sausage. However, you can grind these

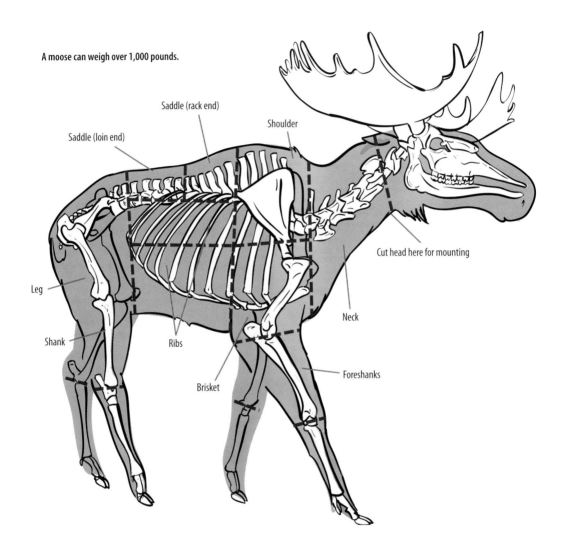

A moose can weigh over 1,000 pounds.

Saddle (rack end)

Saddle (loin end)

Shoulder

Leg

Cut head here for mounting

Shank

Neck

Ribs

Foreshanks

Brisket

smaller pieces for making ground jerky. The hindquarters are often trimmed off the bones, and these will be much larger pieces. They will have enough volume that you can slice strips for making jerky. They are trimmed out in a manner similar to a beef animal carcass, and you can follow the steps previously mentioned to remove them from the carcass.

One important difference between cutting up a cow versus a deer carcass relates to the way in which the animal was dispatched. This most often is a concern when the rifle shot or an arrow tip enters the body of a deer, moose, elk, or other big- or small-game animal.

The lead fragmentation and dispersement of the bullet in the body cavity may be a cause for concern when cutting up the carcass. The extent of lead contamination in muscle tissue may not be a concern if the shot is located in the fore part of the animal. If it entered the rear quarters, there may be more cause for concern. Similarly, arrow tips may break while embedded in the muscles as they are removed.

Before either field dressing the animal or cutting into the carcass, try to identify the entry wound of the projectile and/or any exit point. Any damaged muscle will need to be excised before processing the meat. Generally, a ballistic tip/soft point, rapid-expansion bullet will have the highest fragmentation rate. One study conducted by the Minnesota Department of Natural Resources found that bullet fragments in a carcass could be found between 11 to 14 inches from the exit wound. The study's conclusion was that routine trimming of damaged muscles near the wound likely will not remove all of the bullet fragments.

Fragments left in the carcass, particularly if fairly large, may be a concern during the processing of the meat into jerky. If put through a grinder, these fragments may be further broken up and spread throughout the meat mixture with relatively little indication. Or a small metal piece may pass through all processes only to be found when biting into and chewing the dried jerky.

While these may be extreme and unlikely conditions, you should be aware of them if processing any wild game killed with bullets or arrows.

Small-Game Animals

While big-game animals may offer more substantial fare for jerky making, small-game animals shouldn't be overlooked. These may include rabbits and hare, squirrels, and beaver. There are others, but remember that as you pursue smaller animals, the amount of muscle available for making jerky also decreases. Most will need to be accessed with a hunting license.

Most rabbits and hare are small and often difficult to cut into strips except, perhaps, the loin on a larger animal. The rest can be cut into medallions or into ground meat for jerky.

Beaver may be trapped and meat strips may be cut from the hind leg and loin. The rest is likely to be too small for strips and can be used for ground meat or jerky nuggets.

A more exotic animal, the alligator, has a lean white meat that can be obtained from alligator farms and other legal venues licensed to provide them.

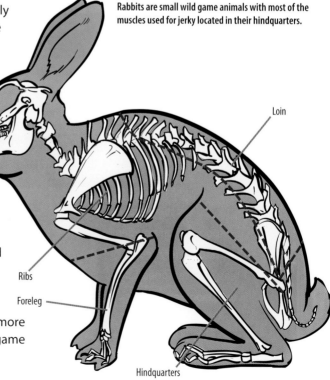

Rabbits are small wild game animals with most of the muscles used for jerky located in their hindquarters.

Loin

Ribs

Foreleg

Hindquarters

CLASSIC VENISON JERKY

2 POUNDS LEAN VENISON, SLICED INTO ¼-INCH-THICK STRIPS

MARINADE

2 tablespoons salt

2 tablespoons soy sauce

1½ tablespoons dark brown sugar

4 cloves garlic, minced

2 teaspoons ground black pepper

In a nonmetallic container, mix the salt, soy sauce, brown sugar, minced garlic, and black pepper. Place the meat strips in the marinade and evenly coat. Place the strips on oven racks or dehydrator trays and refrigerate for 24 hours. Using one of the four methods in Chapter 3 (starting on page 58), dry the meat. Make sure the meat reaches an internal temperature of 160°F. Remove, let cool, and store in sealed jars in the refrigerator.

SOY VENISON JERKY

2 POUNDS LEAN VENISON, SLICED INTO ¼-INCH-THICK STRIPS

MARINADE

¼ cup soy sauce

3 tablespoons steak sauce

1 teaspoon onion powder

1 teaspoon celery seeds

1 teaspoon seasoned salt

¼ teaspoon ground black pepper

In a nonmetallic container, thoroughly mix soy sauce, steak sauce, onion powder, celery seeds, seasoned salt, and black pepper. Place meat strips in a sturdy plastic food bag and pour in the marinade so all the strips are completely covered. Seal the bag and place in the refrigerator for 8 to 10 hours. Using one of the four methods in Chapter 3 (starting on page 58), dry the meat. Make sure the meat reaches an internal temperature of 160°F. Remove, let cool, and store in sealed jars in the refrigerator.

BIG-BATCH VENISON JERKY

5 POUNDS LEAN VENISON, SLICED INTO ¼-INCH-THICK STRIPS

MARINADE

1 cup soy sauce

½ cup Worcestershire sauce

2 tablespoons liquid smoke

½ tablespoon salt

½ tablespoon ground black pepper

In a nonmetallic container, mix the soy sauce, Worcestershire sauce, and liquid smoke. Add the meat strips and coat all sides. Cover and marinate 8 hours or overnight in refrigerator. Drain off the marinade and arrange the strips on oven racks or dehydrator trays. Mix the salt and pepper in a shaker and sprinkle evenly onto one side of strips. Turn over and sprinkle the other side. Using one of the four methods in Chapter 3 (starting on page 58), dry the meat. Make sure the meat reaches an internal temperature of 160°F. Remove, let cool, and store in sealed jars in the refrigerator.

ELK JERKY

4 POUNDS LEAN ELK, SLICED INTO ¼-INCH-THICK STRIPS

MARINADE

1 cup soy sauce

½ cup Worcestershire sauce

1 tablespoon salt

½ cup light brown sugar

1 teaspoon onion powder

½ tablespoon red pepper flakes

In a nonmetallic container, mix the soy sauce, Worcestershire sauce, salt, brown sugar, onion powder, and red pepper flakes until the sugar and salt are dissolved. Add the meat strips, cover the container, and marinate for 36 hours in the refrigerator. Using one of the four methods in Chapter 3 (starting on page 58), dry the meat. Make sure the meat reaches an internal temperature of 160°F. Remove, let cool, and store in sealed jars in the refrigerator.

MOOSE JERKY

2 POUNDS LEAN MOOSE MEAT, SLICED INTO ¼-INCH-THICK STRIPS

MARINADE

2 cups soy sauce

¼ cup honey

1 tablespoon prepared mustard

1 teaspoon onion salt

1 teaspoon garlic salt

In a nonmetallic container, mix the soy sauce, honey, mustard, onion salt, and garlic salt. Add the meat and coat all sides. Cover the meat completely with marinade, cover, and refrigerate for 8 hours or overnight. Using one of the four methods in Chapter 3 (starting on page 58), dry the meat. Make sure the meat reaches an internal temperature of 160°F. Remove, let cool, and store in sealed jars in the refrigerator.

RABBIT JERKY

1 POUND RABBIT MEAT, SLICED INTO ¼-INCH-THICK STRIPS

MARINADE

¼ cup soy sauce

¼ cup Worcestershire sauce

½ teaspoon onion powder

½ teaspoon garlic powder

½ teaspoon seasoned salt

¼ teaspoon ground black pepper

In a nonmetallic container or sealable plastic bag, mix the soy sauce, Worcestershire sauce, onion powder, garlic powder, seasoned salt, and black pepper. Add the strips, coat all strips evenly, cover the container, and refrigerate for 8 hours or overnight. Using one of the four methods in Chapter 3 (starting on page 58), dry the meat. Make sure the meat reaches an internal temperature of 160°F. Remove, let cool, and store in sealed jars in the refrigerator.

BISON JERKY

1 POUND LEAN BISON MEAT, SLICED INTO ¼-INCH-THICK STRIPS

MARINADE

3 tablespoons soy sauce

3 tablespoons Worcestershire sauce

3 tablespoons hoisin sauce

1 tablespoon light brown sugar

1 teaspoon onion powder

1 teaspoon garlic powder

1 teaspoon salt

½ teaspoon ground black pepper

1 teaspoon liquid smoke (optional)

In a nonmetallic container, mix the soy sauce, Worcestershire sauce, hoisin sauce, brown sugar, onion powder, garlic powder, salt, pepper, and liquid smoke (if desired) until the sugar is thoroughly dissolved. Combine the meat strips with the marinade, cover the container, and refrigerate for 8 hours or overnight. Using one of the four methods in Chapter 3 (starting on page 58), dry the meat. Make sure the meat reaches an internal temperature of 160°F. Remove, let cool, and store in sealed jars in the refrigerator.

TERIYAKI BISON JERKY

1 POUND LEAN BISON MEAT, SLICED INTO ¼-INCH-THICK STRIPS

MARINADE

¼ cup soy sauce

½ teaspoon salt

⅛ teaspoon ground black pepper

½ teaspoon ground ginger

2 tablespoons light brown sugar

1 clove garlic, crushed

In a nonmetallic container, thoroughly mix soy sauce, salt, pepper, ginger, sugar, and crushed garlic. Sprinkle one-quarter of the marinade on the bottom of a flat dish. Place one-quarter of the meat in a single layer in the dish. Sprinkle one-quarter of the marinade over that layer. Then place a second meat layer over the first and sprinkle with one-quarter of the marinade, and then place a third meat layer over the second. Coat the top layer with the rest of the marinade, cover the container, and refrigerate for 6 to 12 hours. Using one of the four methods in Chapter 3 (starting on page 58), dry the meat. Make sure the meat reaches an internal temperature of 160°F. Remove, let cool, and store in sealed jars in the refrigerator.

DRY RUB FOR WILD GAME

2 POUNDS WILD GAME, SLICED INTO ¼-INCH-THICK STRIPS

DRY RUB

1 tablespoon brown sugar

2 teaspoons ground black pepper

1 teaspoon garlic powder

½ teaspoon cayenne pepper

In a nonmetallic container, mix the sugar, pepper, garlic powder, and cayenne thoroughly. Rub the slices on all sides with the dry rub. Using one of the four methods in Chapter 3 (starting on page 58), dry the meat. Make sure the meat reaches an internal temperature of 160°F. Remove, let cool, and store in sealed jars in the refrigerator.

EXTRA-SPICY DRY RUB FOR WILD GAME

2 POUNDS WILD GAME, SLICED INTO ¼-INCH-THICK STRIPS

DRY RUB

1 tablespoon granulated white sugar

1 tablespoon onion powder

2 tablespoons garlic powder

2 tablespoons dried thyme

1 tablespoon juniper berries, crushed or minced

1 teaspoon cayenne pepper

In a nonmetallic container, mix the sugar, onion powder, garlic powder, thyme, berries, and cayenne thoroughly. Rub the slices on all sides with the dry rub. Using one of the four methods in Chapter 3 (starting on page 58), dry the meat. Make sure the meat reaches an internal temperature of 160°F. Remove, let cool, and store in sealed jars in the refrigerator.

DRY RUB FOR VENISON/MOOSE/ELK

2 POUNDS VENISON, SLICED INTO ¼-INCH-THICK STRIPS

DRY RUB

2 tablespoons light brown sugar

2 tablespoons ground black pepper

2 tablespoons paprika

2 tablespoons garlic powder

1 tablespoon onion powder

1 teaspoon allspice

1 teaspoon celery seed

¼ cup liquid smoke (optional)

In a nonmetallic container, mix the sugar, pepper, paprika, garlic powder, onion powder, allspice, celery seed, and liquid smoke (if desired) thoroughly. Rub the slices on all sides with the dry rub. Using one of the four methods in Chapter 3 (starting on page 58), dry the meat. Make sure the meat reaches an internal temperature of 160°F. Remove, let cool, and store in sealed jars in the refrigerator.

Chapter 5

FISH AND FOWL JERKY

A variety of fresh and saltwater fish can be used to make jerky. Many domestic fowl and wild waterfowl species can be used as well. As with all birds harvested in the wild, you will need to handle them carefully and keep them cold during any transport.

While you're free to try anything that suits your tastes when it comes to fish, generally fish with firm, low-fat flesh will dry and store better and longer than those carrying more fat. Some fatty fish species, such as salmon, can preserve quite well, as they have the advantage of having boneless fillets that are easily cut into strips. If you are unable to catch or purchase fresh fish, you may be able to use frozen fish if they were properly frozen—meaning frozen while they were still very fresh. This may not be detectable in many frozen food cases, so fresh is always the best first option.

SELECTING AND PROCESSING FISH

Fish jerky has been around for centuries; Native Americans on both coasts of North America smoked and dried salmon for winter use. They sometimes ground it into a powder, which they traded with other tribes. Dried fish was not only a part of the North American diet. Northern European households have a long history of drying codfish as well.

Drying fish for jerky is similar to using meat from land-based animals. The best fish jerky comes from lean-meat fish. Freshwater fish that are lean include walleye, bluegill, crappie, brook trout, bass, and perch. Ocean fish that make good jerky and are relatively low in fat and oil include codfish, flounder, and tuna (if trimmed). It's best to avoid fish species that typically have higher contents of fat and oil, such as catfish, pike, carp, mackerel, and

Fish can be used for jerky. Lean-meat fish such as walleye, bass, northern pike, or bluegill are best because they contain less fats and oils.

whitefish. The high fat and oil content will make them more difficult to dry, and contribute to a shorter shelf life and increased likelihood of the jerky becoming rancid.

In many of these high fat and oil fish species, the main issue is that it is difficult to trim off the fat; it is usually distributed more or less evenly throughout their muscles. These fish, however, can be smoked with excellent results. Even though smoking will help preserve them, they will not be considered jerky.

As a rule, the larger the fish, the larger the fillets will be if properly trimmed out. Larger strips are often easier to slice into strips for jerky. Smaller fish such as bass, perch, sunfish, crappies, and other panfish can be used, but their yield will often be less and the fillets much smaller and harder to work with.

Another consideration in using fish for jerky is the number of bones involved. Salmon, although it contains more fat than several other fish species, can be used quite easily because its fillets are bone-free, and thus it's easy to slice into strips thin enough for proper dehydration.

It is important to keep fish fresh and cool as long as possible after their catch. Keep them in cold water until you are ready to fillet them.

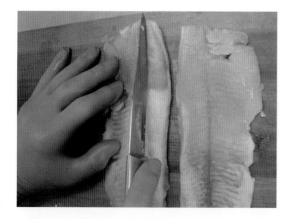

The fillets should be laid out on a clean cutting board. Use fillets that do not contain bones or debone fish before cutting it into strips for jerky.

Slice the fillets into long strips with a sharp-edged knife. They can be placed in a marinade for flavoring, just as for beef, venison, and other meats.

Panfish fillets can often be used whole because they are smaller in size. Larger fillets can be cut into strips.

Processing

Proper handling of any fish you catch, from the time you remove the hook to when you begin to fillet it, is extremely important for good quality meat. Keeping fish alive, fresh, and in cool water until just before cleaning and dressing is the secret to preserving your catch. It will reduce the chance of warm meat, which can become soft and more difficult to slice.

Fish can quickly deteriorate or decompose if not kept cool and fresh. If you plan to use fish to make jerky, you must begin the preservation process from the moment they are caught and removed from their watery habitat until you dry their fillets for jerky. Keep them out of sunlight, avoid bruising them during handling, and keep them cold if making a long return trip to your home, even if they are kept alive.

Dead fish can be placed on ice, but not for an extended period of time unless you fully freeze

Canning or pickling salt is used to cure the fillets. You can add flavors and spices to create different tastes.

If a dry rub is used, first thoroughly mix all ingredients and then spread the dry cure and seasoning mixture over the fish strips. Make sure they are all well covered with the mix.

Place the fish strips in a nonmetallic bowl or pan and layer the seasoned fish strips. Alternate with dry cure mixture, cover, and allow to sit overnight in your refrigerator.

A liquid marinade can also be used. Use the same process to marinate fish that you would use with meat.

Remove the strips and wash off the salt and seasonings after the cure or marinade is done.

Fish can then be dried in an oven or a dehydrator. When it's finished, you should have no moisture on the surface of the fish jerky sticks.

Panfish can be made into jerky. With dehydration and cooking, many pieces will be small because of shrinkage but will be tasty.

them. They will need to be dressed and filleted prior to freezing as well. *Do not* freeze fish for jerky making unless the internal organs have been removed. They will be more difficult to clean after freezing, and it will take additional time to completely cool or freeze a body cavity in which the internal organs are still intact.

Use only the meat from fish that are completely free of parasites, free of slime, and firm without an off odor. If unsure about any possible parasite problems, you can freeze the fish for 48 hours prior to curing or dehydrating to eliminate potential problems.

In almost all fish, the large muscles of the body and tail comprise most of the meat. Fish muscles are often divided into red muscle and white muscle. The red muscles contain many capillaries and appear red because of the high concentration of oxygen-binding pigments. The white muscles are thicker than the red and have a poorer blood supply, which results in fewer oxygen-carrying pigments. The white muscles

Brines

A dry or wet brine can be used for fish. The main reasons to brine fish prior to drying are to enhance flavors from the use of salt and to help hold the meat together. The dissolved salt breaks down some of the proteins in the muscle fibers and causes them to unwind and swell. Then as the meat is dried these protein units bond together again as they shrink and help to hold the meat fibers together. Here are two basic brines for fish jerky; you can choose to use one of the below, or read on for other recipe options. After brining, you can dry the fish using one of the four methods in Chapter 3 (starting on page 58).

DRY BRINE FOR FISH

1 to 2 pounds fish strips

1 cup non-iodized salt

1 cup light brown sugar

Mix the salt and sugar together in a small bowl. Sprinkle a layer of the mixture in nonmetallic container. Roll each fish strip in the dry brine to coat it and place in a container. Do not overlap the strips. Cover the container and refrigerate for 4 to 8 hours.

LIQUID BRINE FOR FISH

1 to 2 pounds fish strips

¼ cup non-iodized salt

2 cups non-chlorinated water

Place the fish strips in a nonmetallic container. In a bowl, thoroughly mix the salt with the water and stir until completely dissolved. Pour the brine over the fish strips until completely covered. Cover the container and refrigerate for 4 to 8 hours. After 2 hours, turn the strips over. When finished, remove from the brine, rinse, and pat dry with paper towels.

tend to be the larger muscles that can be used for jerky.

Before cutting, clean the fish with cold water and remove any blood or other debris that might be attached to the fillets. Cut the fillets into strips ¼ inch thick and place in a nonmetallic dish. You can also use a liquid or dry brine for soaking the fillets until they're ready to dry.

A fillet knife is typically used to clean fresh fish in preparation for cooking or freezing. You also can use it to slice the fillet into strips for making jerky, or you can use a different knife to cut the strips. It doesn't make much difference which knife you use as long as it is sharp and clean. If using the fillet knife, make sure to clean it after you have removed the skin and before you slice them into strips.

If the fillets are large enough, you should cut the strips about ¼ inch thick, ½ inch wide, and 3 to 4 inches in length. Before they are sliced into strips, you can make small slash cuts across the fillets to help any flavorings to penetrate deeper into the flesh.

After using a liquid or dry brine, remove the fish strips from their container and then pat dry with paper towels. Prior to drying the strips, lightly coat each strip on both sides with soy sauce, liquid smoke, or other flavoring to add taste (see below and through page 108 for recipes). Then proceed with drying as for other types of jerky.

Note: Non-iodized salt—pure salt without the addition of iodine—is preferred for brining and is used in the following recipes.

SALMON JERKY

2 POUND BONELESS SALMON FILLETS, SLICED INTO ½- TO ¾-INCH-THICK STRIPS

BRINE
¾ cup non-iodized salt

1½ quarts cold water

MARINADE
1 cup soy sauce

2 tablespoons molasses

2 teaspoons liquid smoke

In a nonmetallic container, mix the salt and cold water. Add the fish strips and marinate for 30 minutes. Then rinse the strips with fresh water and pat dry with paper towels.

In a separate nonmetallic container, mix the soy sauce, molasses, and liquid smoke. Allow the flavors to blend for 30 minutes. Add the salmon strips and coat on both sides, then cover the container and let marinate for 1 hour in the refrigerator, or place in a sealed container and refrigerate 8 hours or overnight for a longer marinating time. Using one of the four methods in Chapter 3 (starting on page 58), dry the fish. Make sure the fish reaches an internal temperature of 145°F rather than the standard 160°F. Check your jerky on the early side as well to make sure it does not end up overly dry. Remove, let cool, and store in sealed jars in the refrigerator.

HONEYED SALMON JERKY

2 POUNDS BONELESS SALMON FILLETS, SLICED INTO ½- TO ¾-INCH-THICK STRIPS

BRINE

¾ cup non-iodized salt

1½ quarts cold water

MARINADE

¼ cup honey

¼ cup rum

1 tablespoon lemon juice

5 whole cloves

5 peppercorns, crushed

1 bay leaf

1 teaspoon salt

In a nonmetallic container, mix ¾ cup of salt and cold water. Add the fish strips and marinate for 30 minutes. Then rinse the strips with fresh water and pat dry with paper towels.

In a separate nonmetallic container, thoroughly mix the honey, rum, lemon juice, cloves, crushed peppercorn, bay leaf, and 1 teaspoon of salt and allow flavors to blend for 30 minutes. Then add the salmon strips, coat both sides in marinade, then cover the container and marinate for 1 hour in the refrigerator. Using one of the four methods in Chapter 3 (starting on page 58), dry the fish. Make sure the fish reaches an internal temperature of 145°F rather than the standard 160°F. Check your jerky on the early side as well to make sure it does not end up overly dry. Remove, let cool, and store in sealed jars in the refrigerator.

MAPLE COD JERKY

1 POUND COD, SLICED INTO ½- TO ¾-INCH-THICK STRIPS

BRINE

¾ cup non-iodized salt

1½ quarts cold water

MARINADE

½ cup maple syrup

1 teaspoon salt

1 teaspoon liquid smoke

½ teaspoon ground
  black pepper

In a nonmetallic container, mix ¾ cup of salt and cold water. Add the fish strips and marinate for 30 minutes. Then rinse the strips with fresh water and pat dry with paper towels.

In a separate nonmetallic container, thoroughly mix the maple syrup, salt, liquid smoke, and pepper. Allow the flavors to blend for 30 minutes. Add the cod strips, cover the container, and let marinate for 1 hour in the refrigerator, or place in a sealed container and refrigerate 8 hours or overnight for a longer marinating time. Using one of the four methods in Chapter 3 (starting on page 58), dry the fish. Make sure the fish reaches an internal temperature of 145°F rather than the standard 160°F. Check your jerky on the early side as well to make sure it does not end up overly dry. Remove, let cool, and store in sealed jars in the refrigerator.

TERIYAKI TUNA JERKY

1 POUND TUNA, SLICED INTO ½- TO ¾-INCH-THICK STRIPS

BRINE

¾ cup non-iodized salt

1½ quarts cold water

MARINADE

¼ cup teriyaki sauce

2 tablespoons water

2 tablespoons light brown sugar

1 teaspoon ground ginger

1 teaspoon salt

½ teaspoon minced garlic

¼ teaspoon dried tarragon

In a nonmetallic container, mix ¾ cup of salt and 1½ quarts cold water. Add the fish strips and marinate for 30 minutes. Then rinse the strips with fresh water and pat dry with paper towels.

In a separate nonmetallic container, mix the teriyaki sauce, 2 tablespoons water, sugar, ginger, salt, garlic, and tarragon. Allow the flavors to blend for 30 minutes. Add the tuna strips, cover the container, and let marinate for 1 hour in the refrigerator, or place in a sealed container and refrigerate 8 hours or overnight for a longer marinating time. Using one of the four methods in Chapter 3 (starting on page 58), dry the fish. Make sure the fish reaches an internal temperature of 145°F rather than the standard 160°F. Check your jerky on the early side as well to make sure it does not end up overly dry. Remove, let cool, and store in sealed jars in the refrigerator.

SPICY FISH JERKY

2 POUNDS BONELESS HALIBUT FILLETS, SLICED INTO ½- TO ¾- INCH-THICK STRIPS

BRINE

¾ cup non-iodized salt

1½ quarts cold water

MARINADE

½ cup tomato sauce

2 tablespoons minced onion

1 tablespoon minced garlic

1 tablespoon salt

1 tablespoon cayenne pepper

1 tablespoon ground black pepper

1 tablespoon dried thyme

1 tablespoon liquid smoke

In a nonmetallic container, mix ¾ cup of salt and cold water. Add the fish strips and marinate for 30 minutes. Then rinse the strips with fresh water and pat dry with paper towels.

In a separate nonmetallic container, mix the tomato sauce, onion, garlic, salt, pepper, thyme, and liquid smoke. Allow the flavors to blend for 30 minutes. Add each fish strip one at a time and coat evenly on both sides. Cover the container and marinate for 1 hour in the refrigerator. Using one of the four methods in Chapter 3 (starting on page 58), dry the fish. Make sure the fish reaches an internal temperature of 145°F rather than the standard 160°F. Check your jerky on the early side as well to make sure it does not end up overly dry. Remove, let cool, and store in sealed jars in the refrigerator.

SEEDY PANFISH JERKY

1 POUND FRESH PANFISH

BRINE
¾ cup non-iodized salt

1½ quarts cold water

MARINADE
¼ cup light brown sugar

¼ cup soy sauce

1 teaspoon minced garlic

1 teaspoon salt

½ teaspoon ginger

¼ cup white sesame seeds

In a nonmetallic container, mix ¾ cup of salt and cold water. Add the fish strips and marinate for 30 minutes. Then rinse the strips with fresh water and pat dry with paper towels.

In a separate nonmetallic container, mix the sugar, soy sauce, garlic, salt, ginger, and sesame seeds and allow the flavors to blend for 30 minutes. Add the fish pieces, cover the container, and let marinate for 1 hour in the refrigerator, or place in a sealed container and refrigerate 8 hours or overnight for a longer marinating time. Using one of the four methods in Chapter 3 (starting on page 58), dry the fish. Make sure the fish reaches an internal temperature of 145°F rather than the standard 160°F. Check your jerky on the early side as well to make sure it does not end up overly dry. Remove, let cool, and store in sealed jars in the refrigerator.

TROUT JERKY

1 POUND FRESH TROUT, SLICED INTO ¼-INCH-THICK STRIPS

BRINE
¾ cup non-iodized salt

1½ quarts cold water

MARINADE
¼ cup soy sauce

1 teaspoon minced garlic

½ teaspoon ground black pepper

In a nonmetallic container, mix ¾ cup of salt and cold water. Add the fish strips and marinate for 30 minutes. Then rinse the strips with fresh water and pat dry with paper towels.

In a separate nonmetallic container, mix the soy sauce, garlic, and pepper in and allow flavors to blend for 30 minutes. Add each fish strip one at a time and coat evenly on both sides. Cover the container and marinate for 1 hour in the refrigerator. Using one of the four methods in Chapter 3 (starting on page 58), dry the fish. Make sure the fish reaches an internal temperature of 145°F rather than the standard 160°F. Check your jerky on the early side as well to make sure it does not end up overly dry. Remove, let cool, and store in sealed jars in the refrigerator.

CATFISH CAJUN JERKY

1 POUND CATFISH, SKINNED AND SLICED INTO ¼-INCH-THICK STRIPS

BRINE

¾ cup non-iodized salt

1½ quarts cold water

MARINADE

½ cup tomato sauce

1 tablespoon minced onion

1½ teaspoons cayenne pepper

1½ teaspoons dried thyme

1½ teaspoons dried basil

1 teaspoon white pepper

1 teaspoon salt

½ teaspoon ground black pepper

½ teaspoon minced garlic

½ teaspoon liquid smoke

In a nonmetallic container, mix ¾ cup of salt and cold water. Add the fish strips and marinate for 30 minutes. Then rinse off all the salt with fresh water and pat dry with paper towels.

In a separate nonmetallic container, mix the tomato sauce, onion, cayenne pepper, thyme, basil, white pepper, salt, black pepper, minced garlic, and liquid smoke and allow flavors to blend for 30 minutes. Add the catfish strips, cover the container, and let marinate for 1 hour in the refrigerator, or place in a sealed container and refrigerate 8 hours or overnight for a longer marinating time. Using one of the four methods in Chapter 3 (starting on page 58), dry the fish. Make sure the fish reaches an internal temperature of 145°F rather than the standard 160°F. Check your jerky on the early side as well to make sure it does not end up overly dry. Remove, let cool, and store in sealed jars in the refrigerator.

SOLEY JERKY

1 POUND SOLE, SLICED INTO ¼-INCH-THICK STRIPS

BRINE

¾ cup non-iodized salt

1½ quarts cold water

MARINADE

¼ cup fresh lemon juice

1 teaspoon prepared mustard

1 teaspoon salt

1 teaspoon dried dill

1 teaspoon minced garlic

1 teaspoon white sugar

¼ teaspoon ground black pepper

In a nonmetallic container, mix ¾ cup of salt and cold water. Add the fish strips and marinate for 30 minutes. Then rinse the strips with fresh water and pat dry with paper towels.

In a separate nonmetallic container, mix the lemon juice, mustard, salt, dill, garlic, sugar, and pepper and allow flavors to blend for 30 minutes. Add the sole strips, cover the container, and let marinate for 1 hour in the refrigerator, or place in a sealed container and refrigerate 8 hours or overnight for a longer marinating time. Using one of the four methods in Chapter 3 (starting on page 58), dry the fish. Make sure the fish reaches an internal temperature of 145°F rather than the standard 160°F. Check your jerky on the early side as well to make sure it does not end up overly dry. Remove, let cool, and store in sealed jars in the refrigerator.

SELECTING AND PROCESSING FOWL

Wild upland game birds and waterfowl, poultry, turkeys, and other avian species have similar muscle and skeletal structures. Like quadrupeds, fowl will differ in size and muscle development depending on several factors including genetics and diet.

Although all birds that are edible can be made into jerky, small birds do not have large enough muscles to create long strips. Wild and domestic turkeys offer more muscle mass in their breasts and thighs for making strips.

Boning out a turkey breast is the first step in using it for jerky. It can be cut into strips whether fresh or partly frozen. Having a partially frozen piece may help in slicing even, lengthwise strips or across the grain for medallions. While chicken breasts are smaller than turkeys, the principle is the same, and they can be processed in the same manner.

Domestically raised ducks and geese may have more fat than those that feed in the wild. This is dependent on their diet more than their genetic differences, although that may have some effect as well. The best jerky to be made from a duck or goose will come from the breast. When filleted from each side, it creates two portions that can be dried. By trimming away the fat, you can cut along the grain and slice it into strips or across the grain for medallions. One alternative is to grind the smaller pieces for ground-meat jerky.

Upland game birds such as quail, partridge, grouse, or doves are generally too small for making strips for jerky. Their small muscles can be sliced into chunks or medallions, or made into ground-meat jerky. Pheasants offer larger muscles. They have lean, white meat, and a typical pheasant can yield enough meat for strips. Licensed game bird farms are an option to acquire these birds if you prefer not to hunt or don't have the opportunity.

Wild or domestically raised turkeys and chickens can be used for jerky meat. The breast meat is best because it contains the least amount of fat and is large enough a cut to slice into strips.

Remove the feathers before you deconstruct the bird (see page 112). Plucking is a useful way if you do not need the skin for any other use.

Although chickens are smaller in size than turkeys, the principle for processing them is the same. Be sure to chill your bird as quickly as possible after removing the feathers.

Flightless bird species such as ostrich and emu are now being commercially raised and may be an option for jerky meat. They typically have lean, dark meat with less fat than beef. An ostrich may reach a weight of 400 pounds, while the smaller emu can weigh 140 pounds. For these birds, the best meat is found in the thighs rather than the breast, which is not as well developed as in birds of flight.

There are some bird health concerns that you should be aware of before using them for jerky or any other food. All wild birds and waterfowl are susceptible to a variety of diseases and parasites just as wild game animals are. These include avian influenza, duck virus enteritis (sometimes referred to as duck plague), avian cholera, botulism, and lead poisoning.

Avian influenza, or bird flu, is an illness caused by several different strains of influenza viruses that adapt to specific hosts. Humans can be affected through contact with an infected bird, especially by handling an infected dead bird or by contact with infected fluids. As of this writing, there have been no reported instances of bird-to-human transmission in the United States. Still, you must be careful when handling wild birds. Be sure your game bird appears healthy before dressing it. Birds affected with avian flu may exhibit symptoms such as a nasal discharge, diarrhea, and a purple discoloration of the wattles, combs, and legs.

Duck virus enteritis is caused by a herpes virus and can be spread through contaminated water or direct contact between birds. It's been reported to have a 90 percent mortality rate when it affects ducks and geese. Listless birds that are unable to fly should be examined closely if shot. There may also be discoloration in the esophagus or blood in the digestive tract that is not attributable to having been caused by hemorrhaging resulting from a gunshot wound.

The breast meat should be sliced to the same thickness as beef or venison, about one-quarter of an inch thick.

The strips should be placed in a nonmetallic bowl. Then you can add the marinade, cover, and refrigerate overnight.

These strips were made with small pieces that could also be ground up to make ground meat jerky.

In the wild, avian cholera is a disease caused primarily by one bacterial strain and is transmitted by direct contact between birds. Humans are not at risk for infection from this bacterial strain but you should wear gloves, wash your hands, and use caution if you handle birds that appear lethargic or fly erratically prior to being shot. Be very cautious about using any easily captured bird for consumption.

Botulism is deadly and can be transmitted to humans. Birds become infected by feeding on invertebrate carcasses that harbor the toxin produced by botulism bacteria. This toxin will attack the bird's nervous system, causing paralysis. Don't eat any bird that displays symptoms such as an inability to propel itself across water or erratic flight movements.

Lead poisoning occurs when wild waterfowl ingest spent lead shot from hunters' guns. Lead shot can be picked up from lake or marsh bottoms or in low feeding areas. Birds exhibiting lead poisoning will have difficulty flying or be unable to fly. They may be so weak that you can easily catch them, or they might have a staggered or unbalanced walk on land. In short, don't use the meat from sick birds or birds that act abnormally for making jerky or any other food.

Processing

As a rule, the largest muscles of any avian species are the pectorals, or breast muscles, and these will yield the most meat for jerky. These muscles make up about 15 to 20 percent of the bird's total weight. They also provide the powerful downstroke of the wings and are the major support for a bird in flight. The supracoracoideus is a muscle located below and in front of the pectoral muscle that raises the wing. Although small, it can be trimmed off and used in ground meat jerky.

Processing wild game birds and waterfowl for jerky is identical to using domestically raised

Test chicken or turkey jerky in the same way you would beef jerky. It should bend but not be so brittle that it breaks or snaps apart.

poultry and fowl. The main differences are the ability to catch the birds and the locale where they are initially processed, whether in the field, in a shed, or purchased at a market. Generally, you will not be able to purchase wild game birds or fresh waterfowl in local markets unless they are specially licensed outlets.

Besides field dressing (if they are harvested in the wild), there are three similar steps used to process domestic birds and wild ones:

- Removing the feathers

- Breaking down the bird carcass

- Chilling and/or cutting it up for use

Removing Feathers

The feathers of game birds and waterfowl will need to be removed before breaking down the carcass. Generally, dry picking of feathers is a preferred method and can be done in the field. The majority of the feathers can be pulled out before the birds are cooled and brought home.

You can also use a scalding water method, which includes heating a tub of water between 155 to 212 degrees Fahrenheit, then dipping the bird into the water from 5 to 10 seconds to loosen the feathers, which you can then pick off with your fingers. Or, you can simply pick the feathers off by hand without scalding the carcass.

Scalding rules:

- Less immersion time is needed when the water temperature is higher.

- Overscalding causes skin to tear and discolor.

Waterfowl feathers, however, present a challenge: their feathers contain natural water-repellant oils that help the bird retain body heat while in the water and prevents water from matting the feathers together, which might prevent flight.

Breaking Down the Carcass and Chilling

The most basic method to butcher birds includes knives for eviscerating and cutting, and perhaps a hatchet and chopping block for removing heads, if you are working with domestic fowl. When hunting, birds should be eviscerated in the field if possible. If the entrails are retained, the internal body heat does not cool and may cause the meat to spoil. Opening the body cavity and removing the internal organs allows air to enter and cool the inside of the carcass.

It's fairly simple to dress your bird for cutting. Use gloves before opening the body cavity with your knife to protect yourself from coming into contact with the blood and organs in case of any disease.

- Begin by cutting off the last two joints of the wing with game shears or a knife.

- Remove any feathers (see page 111) from below the breastbone to the anal opening, and then make a cut through the skin and muscle starting below the breastbone and continuing to the anus.

- Remove the internal organs by pulling them through the opening, taking care not to puncture the intestines and contaminate the interior with fecal matter.

- Remove the oil gland on the top side of the tail bud. This gland contains the oil that birds use to coat their feathers, and it can cause off flavors in the meat if left intact.

- Pull the skin away from the breast muscles and legs. The skin should pull away from the carcass so that you are left with the muscles and bones.

- Remove the head and tail with a game shears. Clean the body cavity with clean, fresh water, then rinse and pat dry. Do not use creek, river, or pond water to clean out the cavity because it likely is not free of contamination.

- After removing all the skin, feathers, internal organs, head, and tail, you are ready to trim the muscles from the skeleton. Place the bird on its back.

- Use a sharp knife to slice the breast halves away from the breastbone. Keep the blade as close to the bone as possible.

- Now work on the legs. Push one leg down to pop the ball-and-socket joint. Then cut through the joint to remove the leg. Repeat this process on the other leg. Cut apart the thighs and drumstick and begin to trim the meat from the bone.

With the two breasts, thighs, and drumsticks removed you will have the largest cuts from which to make jerky strips. The other smaller pieces that are trimmed from the wings can be ground and mixed with other meat you may have available and used for ground meat jerky.

As with all other meats you use, be sure to chill your game bird and waterfowl meat as quickly as possible and keep it cold until it is to be used.

CHICKEN JERKY

1½ POUNDS CHICKEN BREASTS, BONED, SKINLESS, SLICED INTO ¼-INCH-THICK STRIPS

MARINADE

½ cup soy sauce

1 teaspoon lemon juice

½ teaspoon garlic powder

½ teaspoon ground black pepper

¼ teaspoon ground ginger

In a nonmetallic container, mix the soy sauce, lemon juice, garlic, pepper, and ginger. Allow the flavors to blend for 30 minutes. Add the chicken strips, cover the container, and let marinate for 1 hour in the refrigerator, or place in a sealed container and refrigerate 8 hours or overnight for a longer marinating time. Using one of the four methods in Chapter 3 (starting on page 58), dry the meat. Make sure the meat reaches an internal temperature of 165°F rather than the standard 160°F. Remove, let cool, and store in sealed jars in the refrigerator.

TURKEY DELIGHT JERKY

1 POUND TURKEY BREAST MEAT, SLICED INTO ¼-INCH-THICK STRIPS

MARINADE

2 tablespoons soy sauce

¼ cup Worcestershire sauce

¼ teaspoon Tabasco sauce

2 teaspoons light brown sugar

1 tablespoon onion powder

2 teaspoons garlic powder

1 teaspoon salt

1 tablespoon liquid smoke

1 teaspoon mesquite flavoring liquid

In a nonmetallic container, mix the soy sauce, Worcestershire sauce, Tabasco sauce, sugar, onion powder, garlic powder, salt, liquid smoke, and mesquite flavoring in nonmetallic container until the sugar and salt are thoroughly dissolved. Add the turkey strips, cover the container, and marinate in the refrigerator for 8 to 10 hours or overnight. Using one of the four methods in Chapter 3 (starting on page 58), dry the meat. Make sure the meat reaches an internal temperature of 165°F rather than the standard 160°F. Remove, let cool, and store in sealed jars in the refrigerator.

WILD DUCK BREAST JERKY

1 POUND FRESH WILD DUCK BREAST, SLICED INTO ¼-INCH-THICK STRIPS

MARINADE

½ cup soy sauce

½ cup Worcestershire sauce

1 tablespoon honey

2 teaspoons onion powder

2 teaspoons ground black pepper

1 teaspoon red pepper flakes

1 teaspoon liquid smoke

In a nonmetallic container, mix the soy sauce, Worcestershire sauce, honey, onion powder, black pepper, red pepper flakes, and liquid smoke. Add the meat strips and coat evenly. Cover the container and marinate for 4 hours in the refrigerator. Using one of the four methods in Chapter 3 (starting on page 58), dry the meat. Make sure the meat reaches an internal temperature of 165°F rather than the standard 160°F. Remove, let cool, and store in sealed jars in the refrigerator.

PHEASANT BREAST JERKY

1 POUND FRESH PHEASANT BREAST, SLICED INTO ¼-INCH-THICK STRIPS

MARINADE

¼ cup teriyaki sauce

2 tablespoons water

2 tablespoons light brown sugar

1 teaspoon salt

½ teaspoon minced garlic

In a nonmetallic container, mix the teriyaki sauce, water, sugar, salt, and garlic. Allow the flavors to blend for 30 minutes. Add the pheasant strips, cover the container, and let marinate for 1 hour in the refrigerator, or place in a sealed container and refrigerate 8 hours or overnight for a longer marinating time. Using one of the four methods in Chapter 3 (starting on page 58), dry the meat. Make sure the meat reaches an internal temperature of 165°F rather than the standard 160°F. Remove, let cool, and store in sealed jars in the refrigerator.

OSTRICH JERKY

1 POUND OSTRICH BREAST MEAT, SLICED INTO ¼-INCH-THICK STRIPS

MARINADE

½ cup soy sauce

½ cup Worcestershire sauce

½ cup water

½ cup teriyaki sauce

1 cup dry red wine

1½ teaspoons Tabasco sauce

½ teaspoon garlic powder

½ teaspoon ground ginger

½ teaspoon onion powder

1 teaspoon liquid smoke

2 teaspoons light brown sugar

1 teaspoon salt

In a nonmetallic container, mix the soy sauce, Worcestershire sauce, water, teriyaki sauce, red wine, Tabasco sauce, garlic powder, ginger, onion powder, liquid smoke, brown sugar, and salt in nonmetallic container until thoroughly dissolved. Add the ostrich meat, cover the container, and marinate in the refrigerator for 10 to 12 hours. Using one of the four methods in Chapter 3 (starting on page 58), dry the meat. Make sure the meat reaches an internal temperature of 165°F rather than the standard 160°F. Remove, let cool, and store in sealed jars in the refrigerator.

QUAIL NUGGETS

1 POUND FRESH QUAIL, SLICED INTO ¼- TO ½-INCH PIECES

MARINADE

½ cup soy sauce

1 teaspoon lemon juice

½ teaspoon garlic powder

½ teaspoon ground black pepper

In a nonmetallic container, mix the soy sauce, lemon juice, garlic, and pepper. Allow the flavors to blend for 30 minutes. Add the quail pieces, cover the container, and let marinate for 1 hour in the refrigerator, or place in a sealed container and refrigerate 8 hours or overnight for a longer marinating time. Using one of the four methods in Chapter 3 (starting on page 58), dry the meat. Make sure the meat reaches an internal temperature of 165°F rather than the standard 160°F by spot checking two or three of your thickest nuggets. Remove, let cool, and store in sealed jars in the refrigerator.

Chapter 6

VEGAN JERKY, TOFU JERKY, AND PEMMICAN

Although meat from animals or fowl make up the most significant amount of jerky made at home or sold through retail outlets, non-meat products can be made into jerky as well. Vegetarian and vegan jerky is becoming popular with those who are seeking an alternative to animal-sourced proteins. Vegan jerky is one of the easiest foods to make. It is good for eating on a road trip or as a hiking snack because it is easy to store, satisfies hunger, and contains a lot of protein. Proponents of vegan jerky consider it to be a healthier food product than jerky derived from animal- and fowl-sourced meats because it is free of cholesterol and animal fats.

The "meat" in the case of vegan jerky is a combination of textured vegetable proteins often mixed with flavorings and fruit juices, together with gluten and ground flax seeds, which act as binders. Most vegetarian jerky is based on soy protein that is available in granular, flake, and chunk forms. A product referred to as textured vegetable protein is another popular choice. It's made from cooked soy flour that has the fat removed. When it is kept cool and dry, it can be kept almost indefinitely. It rehydrates to a remarkable degree. For example, one cup of textured vegetable protein added to one cup boiling water will become two cups of usable protein.

There are a number of moist soy proteins available that contain no fat or cholesterol; are low in sodium; and are high in protein, fiber, and iron. Some products contain dehydrated onions and peppers, carrageenan (a modified vegetable gum), and perhaps a coloring similar to caramel made from corn syrup. A product containing these ingredients will have a texture similar to raw hamburger. As with other jerky making, a variety of flavors can be created including barbeque, Thai peanut, mesquite, hickory smoked, and hot and spicy teriyaki.

117

VEGAN JERKY (OR SOY PROTEIN JERKY)

The basics of making strips of vegetable-based jerky are similar to meat-based ones. Also, the equipment needed is similar, including knives, drying racks or screens, clean countertops, and mixing bowls.

Perhaps the greatest challenge to making vegetable-based jerky is to get the ingredients to bind together. The vegetable ingredients will not stick together by themselves, so a thickening or mucilaginous agent is needed to hold them together during the drying process. Several foods, such as cooked oatmeal and/or applesauce, will bind well with soy proteins and can be effective.

Oatmeal will bind with soy protein to help create cohesiveness in vegan jerky

Distinct flavors can be made using a variety of spices and seasonings.

Besides binding, the second greatest challenge for successful vegetable-based jerky is to make it tasty. More seasonings are typically needed to enhance the flavor. While salt will be the most commonly used seasoning, others such as pepper, onion, and garlic can also be included in recipes. As with animal-based jerky, your choices are limited only by your imagination.

Similar to meat jerky, vegan or vegetable-based jerky will be marinated. The longer it is immersed in a marinade, the stronger the flavors will be. Marinades used for meat-based jerky can be used for vegan or vegetable-based jerky without compromising your intent.

Developing an acceptable jerky-like texture is probably the third and final challenge when making vegetable-based jerky. Oils can add flavor and will help create a more meat-like texture, but oil makes the jerky more difficult to dry.

Vegan jerky is made from vegetable proteins and doesn't achieve a dark color like meat jerky. It is easy to make and offers an excellent alternative jerky choice.

Temperatures

Because this variety of jerky contains no meat, and therefore no harmful meat microorganisms,

Cranberries, raisins, apples, and other fruits and vegetables can be crushed, squeezed, or pureed to add flavor to soy protein.

the temperature requirements are not as stringent. Unlike jerky made with animal muscle meat, you do not need to reach a high temperature of 160 degrees Fahrenheit. Generally, temperatures between 130 to 145 degrees Fahrenheit will be sufficient to create an acceptable jerky product and may take between 6 to 8 hours to adequately dry. Vegan jerky can be made with a dehydrator, and a standard home oven can be used as your dehydrator if it can dependably hold precise temperatures.

When successfully made, vegetable jerky will dry to the consistency of a cracker. If yours turns out too brittle, it can be rehydrated by soaking it in a marinade for several minutes, and then drying it again until the texture is to your liking. One advantage of rehydrating and drying a second time is that you can add more flavorings and seasonings as well. You can also smoke vegan jerky at either stage to add flavor.

ALMOST-LIKE-MEATLOAF JERKY

1 POUND SOY PROTEIN

MARINADE

2½ cups finely chopped onion

1 tablespoon light brown sugar

½ tablespoon minced garlic

1½ ounces instant oatmeal

½ cup non-chlorinated water, divided

1 tablespoon soy sauce

1 tablespoon rum

1 teaspoon ground black pepper

1 teaspoon salt

1 tablespoon grated green bell pepper

1 teaspoon liquid smoke

In a skillet over low heat, caramelize the onions in brown sugar. When the onions are browned and completely soft, add the garlic and mix thoroughly. Mix the oatmeal with ¼ cup water and let stand. Mix the soy sauce, the remaining ¼ cup water, rum, black pepper, salt, green pepper, and liquid smoke thoroughly and let sit for 15 minutes. In a nonmetallic container, mix the onion, sugar, garlic, and oatmeal mixture with the soy protein, and then mix them together with liquids. Cover the container and marinate for 1 hour in the refrigerator, or leave overnight if a longer marinating time is desired. Remove from the marinade container and form into shapes. Using one of the four methods in Chapter 3 (starting on page 58), dry the jerky. For the best consistency, dry at 130 to 140°F. Check on progress after 4 hours and continue drying as needed until you reach the proper consistency. It should be dried to a crisp-like consistency, similar to a cracker. Store the jerky in an airtight container or sealed plastic bag and refrigerate.

CLASSIC VEGETARIAN JERKY

1 POUND SOY PROTEIN

MARINADE

¼ cup plus 3 tablespoons non-chlorinated water, divided

1½ ounces instant oatmeal

1½ ounces dry onion soup mix

2 tablespoons vegetable or olive oil

1 teaspoon salt

1 teaspoon minced garlic

½ teaspoon liquid smoke

Mix ¼ cup water and the oatmeal together and let sit. Mix the dry onion soup and 3 tablespoons water together. In a nonmetallic container, combine the oatmeal and dry onion soup mixture thoroughly. Stir in the oil, salt, garlic, and liquid smoke, and mix thoroughly. Allow the flavors to blend for 30 minutes. Add the soy protein and mix thoroughly. Cover the container and marinate for 1 hour in the refrigerator, or leave overnight if a longer marinating time is desired. Remove from the marinade container and form into shapes. Using one of the four methods in Chapter 3 (starting on page 58), dry the jerky. For the best consistency, dry at 130 to 140°F. Check on the progress after 4 hours and continue drying as needed until you reach the proper consistency. It should be dried to a crisp-like consistency, similar to a cracker. Store the jerky in an airtight container or sealed plastic bag and refrigerate.

TERIYAKI SOY JERKY

1 POUND SOY PROTEIN

MARINADE

1½ ounces instant oatmeal

¼ cup non-chlorinated water

½ cup teriyaki sauce

½ cup plain, non-spiced applesauce

2 tablespoons olive oil

1 teaspoon minced garlic

1 teaspoon salt

1 teaspoon liquid smoke

1 teaspoon ground black pepper

Mix the oatmeal and water together and let sit for 5 minutes. Add the teriyaki sauce, applesauce, olive oil, garlic, salt, liquid smoke, and pepper. Mix thoroughly and allow the flavors to blend for 15 minutes. Add the soy protein and blend together with liquid mix. Place in a sealed container and marinate for 1 hour in the refrigerator, or leave overnight if a longer marinating time is desired. Remove from marinade container and puree in a blender. Remove and form into shapes. Using one of the four methods in Chapter 3 (starting on page 58), dry the jerky. For the best consistency, dry at 130 to 140°F. Check on the progress after 4 hours and continue drying as needed until you reach the proper consistency. It should be dried to a crisp-like consistency, similar to a cracker. Store the jerky in an airtight container or sealed plastic bag and refrigerate.

TACO SOY JERKY

1 POUND SOY PROTEIN

MARINADE

1¼ ounces taco seasoning

½ cup non-chlorinated water, divided

½ cup salsa

1½ cup instant oatmeal

Thoroughly mix the taco seasoning and ¼ cup of water and let sit 15 minutes. Mash the salsa with spoon or puree in a blender. Mix the oatmeal and the remaining ¼ cup of water together. Blend taco seasoning mix, salsa, and oatmeal into the soy protein. Place in a sealed container and marinate for 1 hour in the refrigerator, or leave overnight if a longer marinating time is desired. Remove from the marinade container and form into shapes. Using one of the four methods in Chapter 3 (starting on page 58), dry the jerky. For the best consistency, dry at 130 to 140°F. Check on the progress after 4 hours and continue drying as needed until you reach the proper consistency. For this jerky, I recommend turning it every hour. It should be dried to a crisp-like consistency, similar to a cracker. Store the jerky in an airtight container or sealed plastic bag and refrigerate.

TOFU JERKY

Tofu is made from coagulating soy milk and then pressing the resulting curd into soft white blocks. By itself, tofu has a subtle flavor that can be enhanced with marinades, flavorings, spices, and other ingredients. Tofu is high in protein and calcium and can make excellent jerky.

Tofu typically comes in two forms: fresh or processed. Fresh tofu is produced directly from soy milk, while processed tofu is made from fresh tofu and generally has a firmer texture. Fresh tofu is generally sold completely immersed in water to help maintain its moisture content.

Fresh tofu is often divided into three main varieties: soft, firm, and extra firm. All three can be used for making jerky, but only the extra firm tofu will have most of the liquid pressed out, which will aid you on the next step.

Use a weight set on top of the tofu block to press out the moisture. This will aid in drying. With much of the moisture removed, the tofu can be cut into strips and processed for jerky. The required drying times will not vary significantly as long as you remove the moisture from your selected tofu before drying. Properly processed tofu jerky will last about one month when stored in a clean container in a cool, dry area.

As with other types of jerky, marinades and smoking are the keys to developing interesting

After draining, place the tofu block on clean, dry paper towels in a deep pan or dish. Cover the tofu completely with the paper towel.

Tofu can be used for vegan jerky making. It can be purchased at most grocery stores. Begin by draining off the liquid from the container.

flavors. Tofu will pick up smoke flavor relatively quickly, and a half-hour smoking will also help remove a bit of moisture.

Temperatures

Just as with soy protein jerky, the temperature requirements are not as stringent as for meat jerky. Generally, temperatures between 130 to 145 degrees Fahrenheit will be sufficient and it may require 6 to 8 hours to adequately dry.

When successfully made, tofu jerky will dry to the consistency of a cracker. If yours turns out too brittle, it can be rehydrated by soaking it in a marinade for several minutes, and then drying it again until the texture is to your liking. One advantage of rehydrating and drying a second time is that you can add more flavorings and seasonings as well. You can also smoke tofu jerky at either stage to add flavor.

Preparing Tofu

To prepare tofu for use in the following jerky recipes, first remove the tofu from the package. Wrap it in paper towels and place on a flat pan or baking sheet. Place a 2-pound weight or heavy dish on top of the tofu block to press out the water. Let sit for 30 minutes. Unwrap from the paper towels and proceed with your recipe.

After the water has been pressed out, the tofu will be ready to cut into strips.

Wrap the tofu in the towel.

Place a 2-pound weight or several heavy dishes on top of the tofu block to press out any water.

Place the pressed tofu on a clean cutting board and carefully slice into ¼-inch-thick strips.

When tofu jerky dries, it can be fragile and may crumble easily. But is a nutritious, easily chewable snack.

ASIAN-STYLE TOFU JERKY

14 OUNCES FIRM TOFU, DRAINED AND SLICED INTO ¼-INCH-THICK STRIPS

MARINADE

½ cup soy sauce

1 teaspoon garlic powder

½ teaspoon black pepper

2 teaspoons white sugar

¼ teaspoon liquid smoke

1 teaspoon flax seeds

½ cup dried cranberries, minced

2 tablespoons light brown sugar

1 tablespoon vegetable oil

1 teaspoon salt

½ teaspoon black pepper

1 sheet of parchment paper

In a nonmetallic container, mix the soy sauce, garlic powder, ½ teaspoon pepper, white sugar, and liquid smoke until the sugar is completely dissolved. In separate nonmetallic bowl, mix the flax seeds, cranberries, brown sugar, vegetable oil, salt, and the remaining ½ teaspoon pepper thoroughly and set aside. Submerge the tofu slices in marinade and coat evenly. Place in a sealed container and marinate for 1 hour in the refrigerator, or leave overnight if a longer marinating time is desired. Remove the strips from the marinade and place on parchment paper. Sprinkle the flax seeds, cranberries, brown sugar, oil, salt, and pepper mixture on top of strips. Turn over and coat the second side. Using one of the four methods in Chapter 3 (starting on page 58), dry the jerky. For the best consistency, dry at 145°F. Turn the strips over every 2 hours. Check on the progress after 4 hours and continue drying as needed until you reach the proper consistency. Tofu jerky is dry when you press one piece between your fingers but it does not break. You can take one piece apart to determine whether enough moisture has been removed. Store the jerky in an airtight container, sealed plastic bag, or refrigerate.

BARBECUE TOFU JERKY

14 OUNCES FIRM TOFU, DRAINED AND SLICED INTO ¼-INCH-THICK STRIPS

MARINADE

2 tablespoons light brown sugar

2 tablespoons white sugar

1 tablespoon vegetable oil

¼ cup minced onion

¼ cup ketchup

2 tablespoons cider vinegar

2 tablespoons Worcestershire sauce

2 teaspoons ground ginger

1 teaspoon salt

1 teaspoon minced garlic

1 teaspoon Dijon mustard

1 teaspoon liquid smoke

½ teaspoon ground black pepper

⅛ teaspoon cayenne pepper

In a preheated skillet over medium heat, combine the sugars, oil, and onion in a hot pan. Stir, reduce heat, and cook until onions caramelize. In a nonmetallic container, thoroughly mix the ketchup, vinegar, Worcestershire sauce, ginger, salt, garlic, mustard, liquid smoke, black pepper, and cayenne pepper. Allow the flavors to blend for 15 minutes. Mix with the onions and puree in blender. Place the tofu strips in a rimmed pan and pour the marinade over the top. Turn the strips over to coat evenly. Cover and marinate for 1 hour in the refrigerator, or leave overnight if a longer marinating time is desired; turn the strips over occasionally. Using one of the four methods in Chapter 3 (starting on page 58), dry the jerky. For the best consistency, dry at 145°F. Turn the strips over every 2 hours. Check on the progress after 4 hours and continue drying as needed until you reach the proper consistency. Tofu jerky is dry when you press one piece between your fingers but it does not break. You can take one piece apart to determine whether enough moisture has been removed. Store the jerky in an airtight container, sealed plastic bag, or refrigerate.

FRUITY TOFU JERKY

14 OUNCES FIRM TOFU, DRAINED AND SLICED INTO ¼-INCH-THICK STRIPS

MARINADE

½ cup dried cranberries, minced

1¼ cups orange juice

½ cup onion, chopped

2 tablespoons light brown sugar

2 tablespoons white sugar

1 tablespoon vegetable oil

1 teaspoon salt

½ teaspoon ground black pepper

Rehydrate the cranberries in the orange juice. Cook the onion, brown sugar, and white sugar over medium heat until evenly browned and caramelized but not burnt. Add the cranberries, oil, salt, and pepper, and simmer for 2 minutes. Cool and allow flavors to blend for 15 minutes. Drain off the liquid and puree in the blender until completely smooth. Place the tofu strips in a rimmed pan and pour the marinade over the top. Turn the strips over to coat evenly. Cover and marinate for 1 hour in the refrigerator, or leave overnight if a longer marinating time is desired; turn the strips over occasionally. Using one of the four methods in Chapter 3 (starting on page 58), dry the jerky. For the best consistency, dry at 145°F from start to finish. Turn the strips over every 2 hours. Check on the progress from time to time, and continue drying as needed until you reach the proper consistency. Tofu jerky is dry when you press one piece between your fingers but it does not break. You can take one piece apart to determine whether enough moisture has been removed. Store the jerky in an airtight container, sealed plastic bag, or refrigerate.

PEMMICAN

Pemmican is a mixture of dried meat, fat, and often dried fruits for added nutrition and flavor. Its historical roots go back millennia, and early Native Americans likely introduced it to European settlers. It's a high-energy form of jerky that can provide a dense, nutritionally satisfying snack in a small, easy-to-carry form. It is an ideal companion for trail hiking, biking, or for cooking with other foods. It is lightweight, easy to handle, and easy to make.

Pemmican is typically made using lean meat from cows, moose, deer, or elk and from cuts found in the round or rump. It is best not to use pork or bear meat for pemmican because the soft fats they contain can become rancid more quickly than harder fats.

Making Pemmican

To make pemmican, start with between 2 to 6 pounds of meat. If you are using beef, this can be the eye of round, the rump, or even meat used for steaks. You may want to start with a half-batch for your first attempt to experience how the process works.

A variety of ingredients can be used to make pemmican including cranberries and dried fruits.

A typical pemmican recipe might include:

- 4 cups dried meat (it may take 1 to 2 pounds of raw meat to make a cup)

- 3 cups dried fruit such as cranberries, dates, apricots, or apples

- 2 cups rendered fat

The meat used in pemmican should be dehydrated into jerky using the steps mentioned earlier in this book. This dried jerky can be broken into small pieces or pulverized into a powdery mix using with a food processor, or by hand, such as with a mortar and pestle.

How to Render Fat

You should use beef fat for making pemmican. If purchasing fat at a grocery store, butcher market, or other food venue, be sure it is human-consumption-grade and not the type of fat used for bird feeders. Vegetable products such as commercial shortenings can be used as well but may not provide the same flavor or consistency. You want a hard fat such as that found in beef. Pork fat is too soft to make good pemmican because it can go rancid quickly.

The fat will need to be rendered before it is used in pemmican. This simply means that the solid, white fat needs to be heated until it turns into liquid, as that is what will be added to the pemmican mix. It may take about 3 to 4 pounds of beef fat to render 2 cups of liquid fat.

After securing the proper quantity of fat, cut it into ½-inch cubes and place in a skillet at a low to medium setting. Be sure to use a cover over the hot pan, as fat can spatter as it cooks. The spattering is a result of water cooking out of the fat. Also, be sure to keep your hands clear of the cooking fat and make certain children are not around the stove or are not

To render fat, start with large pieces of beef fat.

Slice the fat into ½-inch squares. Dicing it will expose more surface area from which water can escape during heating.

Place the fat cubes in a warm pan and raise the stove temperature to medium to high heat. Cover the pan to prevent spattering as the fat cooks.

As the fat starts to cook, carefully lift the lid and stir the cubes around.

The fat will crackle and spatter as the water it contains is cooked away.

After the fat is done cooking, remove any leftover solids.

Use a fine-wire strainer and pour the liquid fat through it to remove any small bits of residue left.

Pour the hot liquid fat into a heat-resistant glass cup or bowl

able to reach the handle of the hot pan. Hot fat causes very severe burns if it comes in contact with your skin! Wear a cooking glove when you stir the fat.

The fat will slowly render and any residue will float to the top. Allow the fat to simmer for 3 minutes, which will make sure all the water has been driven out. It is important to remove all water from the fat to improve its long-term storage prospects. However, it's a balancing act. You don't want to burn the liquid fat or it will acquire a burnt flavor.

Drain the fat through a fine-mesh sieve or screen into a heat-resistant bowl or cookware to remove any solid residue. This liquid fat, also known as rendered fat, can now be poured over the powdered mixture. It should soak into the meat, giving it a slightly moist texture. If too much fat is added, it will become wet and runny. If too little is added, the meat will be too dry. If either situation happens, you can add more dry meat to the too-wet batch until it reaches the desired consistency, or you can add more fat to moisten up a too-dry mixture.

Basic Pemmican Procedure

1. Use all good sanitation practices before beginning and during this process.

2. Cut the meat into ⅛-inch strips so they will be flat and thin for drying. Cut across the grain if planning to grind the dried pieces.

3. Place the meat on a rack or screen above a tray of tinfoil to catch the drippings. Or, place on racks of a dehydrator and heat to 165°F for 6 to 8 hours.

4. If using an oven, allow air to circulate by cracking the door open about 2 inches or until the first stop. Monitor the meat as it cooks and do not allow it to become too done. The pieces will decrease in size as they lose moisture.

5. Remove dehydrated pieces from the dehydrator or oven after drying and allow to cool.

6. Place pieces in a meat grinder or food blender. If using a blender, grind until almost a powder consistency. You can also use a mortar and pestle to grind the pieces into a powder, although this requires patience and some arm and wrist strength.

7. Add dried berries such as blueberries, cranberries, dried figs, or others to taste.

8. Place the powdered meat and berries in a mixing bowl and add the rendered fat. It should be in liquid form for easier mixing. If it has solidified, place in cooking pan and heat until it is liquid again, but do not let it simmer.

9. Form the mixture into squares, balls, or bars. You may want to use cupcake forms or breadstick molds to help shape it.

10. Place in the refrigerator in covered containers and let cool.

Place your dried meat in a food processor and grind it to a powder.

You can use jerky that has already been made for use in pemmican and eliminate the first five steps above. Pemmican that contains only dried meat, fat, and dried fruit has been found to remain shelf stable for a long time if it is kept dry. Any moisture contact can quickly spoil it. For long-term storage, you may want to vacuum-seal it to keep out potential contamination from insects or moisture. If you add nuts to your mixture, be aware that the pemmican may become less stable because the nuts may go rancid if not kept in a cool environment.

You can add berries or dried fruit either in the food processor and grind them into finer pieces or after the ground meat has been placed in a nonmetallic container or bowl. They can then be mixed in before shaping into pieces.

Pour in the rendered fat.

Mix thoroughly.

Form pemmican into desired shapes such as squares, balls, or bars.

You can also form pemmican in cupcake molds. Then place it, covered, in your refrigerator and let cool before serving.

CURRANT PEMMICAN

6 cups jerky, ground into powder

4 cups currants, dried and diced

¾ cup rendered beef fat

In a nonmetallic container, mix the ground jerky with currants. Slowly add the melted liquid fat. Stir until mixed thoroughly. Shape into small balls or sticks. Store in an airtight container or sealable plastic bags. Refrigerate.

MAPLE SUGAR PEMMICAN

2 pounds jerky, ground into powder

1¼ cups maple sugar

¼ pound seedless raisins

¼ pound dried cranberries

1 cup rendered beef fat

In a nonmetallic container, mix the ground jerky, maple sugar, raisins, and cranberries. Stir the rendered fat into the jerky mixture while it's still liquid. Cool and remove from the container. Shape into small balls or sticks. Store in airtight container or sealable plastic bags. Refrigerate.

HONEY NUT PEMMICAN

2½ cups chopped walnuts

2½ cups seedless raisins

4 cups jerky, ground into powder

2½ cups honey

Grind the walnuts and raisins in a food processor. In a nonmetallic container, thoroughly mix the powdered jerky with the walnuts and raisins. Gradually stir in the honey and mix thoroughly to bind together. Pour into a cupcake mold that is greased or lined with wax paper to a depth of ¾ inch. Place in the refrigerator for 2 hours. Remove and wrap each piece in food-grade freezer, wrapping, or wax paper. Place in sealable plastic bag, or vacuum-pack in individual bags, then refrigerate.

CHERRY NUT PEMMICAN

1 pound jerky, ground into powder

½ cup dried cherries, chopped

½ cup walnuts, chopped

1 cup rendered beef fat

In a nonmetallic container, thoroughly mix the ground jerky with chopped cherries and walnuts. Stir in the rendered fat. Cool and remove from the container, place in small cupcake-like molds, and let harden. Remove and wrap each piece in food-grade freezer or wrapping paper or wax paper. Place in a sealable plastic bag, vacuum-pack in individual bags, or refrigerate.

GLOSSARY

cross-contamination: The transfer of harmful bacteria from one food to another, particularly involving raw meats, vegetables, cutting boards, and utensils if not handled properly.

cube: To cut meat into small squares.

cure: Any process that preserves meat or fish by salting or smoking, which may be aided with preservative substances. Also refers to the mix used for preserving the food.

dehydrate: To remove water or moisture from food to preserve it.

dehydrator: An appliance designed to remove water from foods.

dry rub: A spice and/or herb mixture that is added to the surface of foods before cooking.

extruder: A mechanism through which food is pushed to create desired shapes.

field dress: To remove the internal organs of hunted game animals, birds, or fowl.

fillet: To slice meat from bones or other cuts. Also refers to boneless slices of meat that form portion cuts.

flank: A cut of a quadruped that includes the abdominal muscles.

forequarter: The anterior portion of a carcass side such as the front shoulder.

grinder: A mechanical device that crushes and breaks up meat pieces into small fibers.

hindquarters: The posterior portion of the carcass side.

jerky: A nutrient-dense meat- or soy protein-based food product that has been made lightweight by drying.

liquid smoke: The substance produced from smoke that is condensed, then cooled to form a concentrated liquid for use in flavoring foods.

marbling: The streaks and veins of fat interlacing meat cuts.

marinade: A sauce in which meat or vegetables are soaked before cooking to add flavor.

marinate: To soak foods such as meat or vegetables in a liquid mixture (or marinade) of various flavors.

rehydrate: To restore the moisture to a previously dried food.

render: To melt down fat.

round: A muscle structure found in the rear leg of quadrupeds.

shelf safe: The ability of preserved or processed foods to survive long periods on home or store shelves without spoiling.

side: One matched forequarter and hindquarter, or one-half of a meat animal carcass.

silverskin: The thin, white, opaque layer of connective tissue found on certain cuts of meats, usually inedible.

slicer: A mechanical device that cuts varying widths of foods such as meats, cheeses, or vegetables.

smoke: To flavor, cook, or preserve food by exposing the surface to smoke from a smoldering wood material.

suet: The raw fat found around the kidneys and loins in beef that is used to make tallow.

tallow: The rendered form of beef fat.

METRIC EQUIVALENTS AND CONVERSION

Conversions between US and metric measurements will be somewhat inexact. It's important to convert the measurements for all of the ingredients in a recipe to maintain the same proportions as the original.

General Formula for Metric Conversion

Ounces to grams	multiply ounces by 28.35
Grams to ounces	multiply grams by 0.035
Pounds to grams	multiply pounds by 453.5
Pounds to kilograms	multiply pounds by 0.45
Cups to liters	multiply cups by 0.24
Fahrenheit to Celsius	subtract 32 from Fahrenheit temperature, multiply by 5, then divide by 9
Celsius to Fahrenheit	multiply Celsius temperature by 9, divide by 2, then add 32

Approximate Metric Equivalents by Volume

US	Metric
1 teaspoon	5 milliliters
1 tablespoon	15 milliliters
¼ cup	60 milliliters
½ cup	120 milliliters
1 cup	230 milliliters
1½ cups	360 milliliters
2 cups	460 milliliters
4 cups (1 quart)	0.95 liters
1.06 quarts	1 liter
4 quarts (1 gallon)	3.8 liters

Approximate Metric Equivalents by Weight

US	Metric
0.035 ounce	1 gram
¼ ounce	7 grams
½ ounce	14 grams
1 ounce	28 grams
16 ounces (1 pound)	454 grams
1.1 pounds	500 grams
2.2 pounds	1 kilogram

US	Metric
1 gram	0.035 ounce
50 grams	1.75 ounces
100 grams	3.5 ounces
500 grams	1.1 pounds
1 kilogram (1000 g)	2.2 pounds

Weight Conversion of Common Ingredients

1 pound salt = 1½ cups
1 ounce salt = 2 tablespoons
1 pound sugar = 2¼ cups
1 ounce cure = 1½ tablespoons

Conversion from Ounces to Tablespoons

¼ ounce = 1¼ tablespoons
½ ounce = 2½ tablespoons
¾ ounce = 3¾ tablespoons
1 ounce = 5 tablespoons
2 ounces = 10 tablespoons
3 ounces = 15 tablespoons
4 ounces = 20 tablespoons

Equivalent Measures and Weights

3 teaspoons = 1 tablespoon
4 tablespoons = ¼ cup
16 tablespoons = 1 cup
2 cups = 1 pint
4 cups = 1 quart
2 pints = 1 quart
4 quarts = 1 gallon
16 ounces = 1 pound

RESOURCES

Academy of Nutrition and Dietetics and ConAgra Foods' public awareness website.
www.homefoodsafety.org

Examining Variability Associated with Bullet Fragmentation and Deposition in White-Tailed Deer and Domestic Sheep. Minnesota Department of Natural Resources.
www.dnr.state.mn.us/hunting/lead/short-summary.html

Food Safety Guidelines, North Dakota State University.
www.ag.ndsu.nodak.edu/pubs/yf/foods/fn572.pdf

Food Safety of Jerky, United States Department of Agriculture, Food Safety and Inspection Service, 1998.
www.fsis.usda.gov/wps/wcm/connect/32da4779-ba5e-4d7b-ad5a-2ad8a13aad1e/Jerky_and_Food_Safety.pdf?MOD=AJPERES

Hasheider, Philip. *The Complete Book of Butchering, Smoking, Curing and Sausage Making, How To Harvest Your Livestock & Wild Game.* Voyageur Press, 2010.

Hasheider, Philip. *The Hunter's Guide to Butchering, Smoking & Wild Game & Fish.* Voyageur Press, 2013.

Kendall, Pat, *Jerky: Potential Source of E. coli Infections.* Colorado State University Cooperative Extension, 1997.
www.ext.colostate.edu/pubs/foodnut/09311.html

National Center for Home Food Preservation, University of Georgia, provides access to the most reliable information available concerning food safety and food quality. http://nchfp.uga.edu

Safefood News. Colorado State University Cooperative Extension Service, Vol. 3, No. 3, Summer 1998.

United States Department of Agriculture Food Standards and Labeling Policy Book.
Washington, D.C.: USDA, 2003. www.fsis.usda.gov/Labeling_Policy_Bok_082005.pdf

ACKNOWLEDGMENTS

I wish to thank my wife, Mary, for her constant support and allowing me to commandeer the kitchen for photos and testing. Our son, Marcus, took most of the photos that appear, making this his sixth book with photographs for Voyageur Press. Our daughter, Julia, is the real cook in the family and provided timely advice on a number of points.

I offer a special thank-you to my editor, Thom, who became a great advisor and sounding board as we worked through the manuscript and photos. His patience, advice, and unique Piedmont-region perspective was very helpful to this Midwesterner. He helped to strengthen the content and clarity of this book to achieve its purpose.

ABOUT THE AUTHOR

Philip Hasheider is a fifth-generation farmer who has combined his interests in production agriculture and history to write twenty books. *The Complete Book of Jerky* is his seventh book for Voyageur Press; his full list includes *The Hunter's Guide to Butchering, Smoking & Curing Wild Game & Fish*; *The Complete Book of Butchering, Smoking, Curing, and Sausage Making*; and *How To Harvest Your Livestock & Wild Game*. His diverse writings and essays have appeared in numerous local, regional, national, and international publications. He was the writer for the 2008 *Wisconsin Local Food Marketing Guide* for the Wisconsin Department of Agriculture, Trade, and Consumer Protection that received the 2009 Wisconsin Distinguished Document Award from the Wisconsin Library Association, and the national 2010 Notable Government Documents Award from the American Library Association. He is a three-time recipient of the Book of Merit Award presented by the Wisconsin Historical Society and Wisconsin State Genealogical Society. He lives with his wife, Mary, on their farm in the Honey Creek Valley, Wisconsin, where they pasture-graze beef and he continues to write. They have two children, Marcus and Julia.

INDEX